After 35+ years in F500 sales, Rick Wong has experienced and observed what we present in *Selling with Noble Purpose*. Salespeople who are consistently top performers are universally driven by the joy of helping and relating with people. Noble intent fuels their competitive nature—not money. It's a refreshing read from someone who spent a career in the trenches.

Lisa Earle McLeod,
Author of *Selling with Noble Purpose* &
***Leading with Noble Purpose*,**
President, McLeod & More

Salespeople and entrepreneurs in the B2B world frequently fail because they focus efforts on a generic institutional sale, resulting in an inability to break through and connect with potential customers. Rick provides a framework for how to reorient your efforts to reach the key people inside targeted businesses with authentic communications that they will appreciate.

David Meerman Scott,
Sales and marketing strategist and author of ten books
including *The New Rules of Sales and Service*

Technology has changed the way we find customers and how we help them find us, as I write about in *The Wish*. However, while the digital marketplace helps us to reach more customers, it doesn't eliminate the need for a personal connection. People still choose to do business with people they trust. Rick Wong shares an important framework for maintaining focus on the people side of selling, even in today's technology driven world. Sound insight and a competitive edge are to be gained by reading this new classic sales book, *Winning Lifelong Customers*.

Elinor Stutz, CEO of SmoothSale™ and
author of *Smooth Selling, Hired*,
***Inspired Business, The Wish*, and more**

After more than 35 years of successful sales, marketing, executive management, and entrepreneurial pursuits, Rick Wong shares that the best salespeople are driven by helping and relating to others. In *Winning Lifelong Customers* he introduces a simple framework founded on the principle that people make business decisions for personal reasons. His principles are aligned with BNI's philosophy that Giver's Gain® and that success comes to those who help others. A great read.

Dr. Ivan Misner,
Founder of BNI and NY Times bestselling author

In *Winning Lifelong Customers*, Rick Wong lays out a very usable framework for doing business on a personal level. This is a timely book in today's global economy since other cultures, such as China and other emerging countries, demand personal connection before any business can be done. A good read for business people, in general, and certainly those who plan to do business in cultures that prioritize relationship over product.

Amy Karam, Author of *The China Factor*

Rick Wong has written a book that reads effortlessly and yet is packed with real world how-to nuggets of information for the most-seasoned salespeople and those just starting their careers. A practical, relevant guide that I will return to often. It will become a well-used dog-eared resource!

Lisa Hufford,
Author of *Navigating the Talent Shift*, CEO
Simplicity Consulting – former Fortune 100 Sales Executive

David Nilsson and I wrote, *Making the Jump into Small Business Ownership*, which teaches people how to successfully transition into self-employment. Today, I help clients match small business opportunities to their personal strengths and passions. Among the many skills needed by business owners is sales and marketing. In *Winning Lifelong Customers with The Five Abilities*, Rick Wong offers a sales framework learned over his successful 35+ year career. His structured method is accessible to all and yet comprehensive in addressing complex sales challenges we all face. A great read.

Jeffry Levy,
Author of *Making the Jump into Small Business Ownership*,
President, JL Consulting Services, Inc. dba
The Entrepreneurs Source

I'm glad that Rick has decided to share his knowledge and experiences in this book. The framework he developed while selling HP computers into an IBM stronghold—Boeing Commercial Airplane Group, won us a lot of new business. It will be a helpful read for any salesperson or sales manager, not to mention the many of us who count on successful salespeople—pretty much anyone in business.

Irene Bjorklund,
President/CEO, T-Bar Construction – Former Area
General Manager, Hewlett-Packard, Northwest Area

A private tour of a salesman's mind… retold in a structured manner, simple to learn, yet sophisticated enough to deal with advanced sales situations. Rare to see complex sales situations structured into such a learnable, simple, and systematic style. A real-life journey of a self-made, successful sales professional.

Alex Butt, Founder & Chief Revenue Office,
Glides Consulting Partners – Culture Transformation
Specialists, Singapore – former Fortune 100 Sales Executive

Rick and I met while doing business in 2000. I was an executive decision-maker—he managed the people selling to me. That business relationship became a friendship that will continue beyond retirement. *The Five Abilities* is the framework for how Rick does business, one I found very effective leading to win-win opportunities, and how he coaches others to sell. A good read.

Jim Totton, Vice President & General Manager,
Platforms Business Unit at Red Hat.
Former Vice President, Software at Dell Computers

WINNING LIFELONG CUSTOMERS

WITH

THE FIVE ABILITIES®

RICK WONG

Copyright © 2017 by Rick Wong. All rights reserved.

No part of this publication may be reproduced, stored in a retrieval system, or transmitted in any form or by any means, electronic, mechanical, photocopying, recording, scanning, or otherwise, without the prior written permission of the author(s).

Limit of Liability/Disclaimer of Warranty: While the publisher and author have used their best efforts in preparing this book, they make no representations or warranties with respect to the accuracy or completeness of the contents of this book and specifically disclaim any implied warranties of merchantability or fitness for a particular purpose. No warranty may be created or extended by sales representatives or written sales materials. The advice and strategies contained herein may not be suitable for your situation. You should consult with a professional when appropriate. Neither the publisher nor the author(s) shall be liable for any loss of profit or any other commercial damages, including but not limited to special, incidental, consequential, personal, or other damages.

Winning Lifelong Customers With the Five Abilities
By Rick Wong

1. BUS041000 BUSINESS & ECONOMICS / Management
2. BUS058010 BUSINESS & ECONOMICS / Sales & Selling / Management
3. BUS058000 BUSINESS & ECONOMICS / Sales & Selling / General

Hardcover ISBN: 978-1-935953-73-9
Paperback ISBN: 978-1-935953-74-6

Cover design by Lewis Agrell

Printed in the United States of America

Authority Publishing
11230 Gold Express Dr. #310-413
Gold River, CA 95670
800-877-1097
www.AuthorityPublishing.com

DEDICATION

Thanks to...

...my foundation, Marilyn,
who agreed to marry me in 1981.
My best sale ever. Thank God.

...my future, Bobby and Jacqui,
who make me proud every day
as I learn fathering on the job.

...Mom and Dad,
I feel your presence every day—
I hope I make you smile.

...the patience, persistence,
and push-back from all of the above.
I am blessed beyond words.

ACKNOWLEDGEMENTS

I need a book to thank all who helped me get to this point in my life with a positive outlook and a ton of faith. To all of my family, friends, and co-workers who I'm blessed to learn from—thank you.

Family – My dad is my role model even though he died when my brother and I were nine and ten. My mother was the most caring person ever, but raising two boys alone was hard. We had no money and yet we were provided for. Many aunts and uncles stepped up and were there every day. Auntie Priscilla, my mom's sister—my second mother. Tough as nails; hard to please—she thickened my skin in all the right ways. Uncle Percy, my mom's brother, and Uncle Way, Priscilla's husband, were there when my mom needed a man's touch. Whether teaching us sports, discipline, fetching us from the principal's office, or just being a role model, they were there. Uncle Joe, Auntie Jackie, Uncle Ro, and Auntie Bertha were always there to support my mom when she needed a much-earned break from two rambunctious boys.

Teachers – My sixth-grade teacher Tom Schwerin taught me guitar, which changed my life. The guitar helped pay for college, helped make friends, helped my wife take interest in me, and is a joy I will have for the rest of my life. Helen Mason—high school counselor during the years I was still pouting about my dad's passing. She drilled into me that good things would happen, and good people would be attracted to me, if I got up off my butt and fought for myself. Father McMurtry taught me the same through scripture; 2 Thessalonians 3:10 – "...the one who is unwilling to work shall not eat."

Brother from another mother – Jeff Jenkins and I were college roommates and we've been best friends since. Jeff wakes up every morning with a positive outlook even when things aren't going well. He is the embodiment of what my teachers and pastor taught me. His family showed me a different culture than the Chinese household I came from where good could always be better. With the Jenkins, every day was great. The balance of those two cultures made me better.

Sister from another mother – Candace Grisdale and I met when we were youngsters in an HP office full of seasoned veterans. Our sibling rivalry drove us to perform better, learn faster, and to help the new youngsters coming in behind us. She still kicks me when I need it.

Mentors and managers - I had eleven managers in my thirty-three-year corporate career. I also had six mentors, three women and three men, counting my aunt Priscilla. Jim Kreiter was my first sales manager who taught me the foundational principle of *The Five Abilities*®. Irene Bjorklund mentored me about how systematization would help me be more efficient and effective. Richard Fade taught me to push the creative boundaries when current practices stalled. Steven Guggenheimer (Guggs) taught me to see the big heart that is often hidden inside high IQ, hard-charging leaders.

Lastly, when I started *The Five Abilities*, LLC, I was met with open arms by people who wanted to help with no expectation of anything in return. Andrea Sittig-Rolf, CEO of Blitz Masters and author of five books on selling, gave me great insight into the world of consulting and authoring. Jeff Rogers, CEO of OneAccord Partners, an amazing example of servant leadership, who helped me to see the realities of the consulting world. Lisa Hufford, CEO of Simplicity Consulting, is a peer mentor and a role model for how to turn personal, family priorities into an ultra-successful business that prioritizes the well-being of its people. Dave Fester kick-started my marketing with web development and logo design. Dana Manciagli and I were peers at Microsoft but we're better friends today. She's ahead of me in this entrepreneurial journey and is always willing to share her learnings. James Pinckney and I were VPs at Microsoft but we have also become closer friends and peer mentors since.

I've been blessed. I'm not famous but I'm living the American Dream and much of the credit goes to the many great people around me. I hope this book helps you as much as they've all helped me.

CONTENTS

CHAPTER 1
WINNING LIFELONG CUSTOMERS

Winning lifelong customers is the lifeblood of successful enterprise selling. This once meant simply winning long-term business with a company. However, in today's mobile and global economy, we need to augment the meaning to emphasize individual decision-makers and influencers, because more than ever before success is about selling to and working with the *people* who choose to be our lifelong customers—no matter where they choose to lead and make buying decisions.

Companies don't make decisions—people do, and *people make business decisions for personal reasons.* This is the foundation of modern selling and *The Five Abilities*® sales

> **People make business decisions for personal reasons.**

framework. Too often, salespeople, sales managers, and marketing managers fail to consider those personal reasons, resulting in—at best—incomplete proposals. Sales productivity diminishes because too much time is devoted to pitching the academic and analytic reasons why companies need a product or service. Winning lifelong customers requires that we deliver value to the company *and* the people making decisions, and one does not necessarily get you the other.

Even though you know that winning lifelong customers is the lifeblood of enterprise selling, have you ever gotten to the end of a planning session thinking, "What do I do now?" Have you had those long days when you know you should be in front of the customer but you're thinking, "What do I do now?" When you're having trouble getting past a gatekeeper, are you able to identify an immediate best next action or are you sometimes stuck asking, "What do I do now?"

The Five Abilities gives you a clear set of targets so you can immediately choose your best next actions. You'll never be left asking yourself, "What do I do now?" without having a framework to answer that question quickly and correctly. *The Five Abilities* sales framework gives you a blueprint to construct the sales actions that best address the five things that decision-makers most need when deciding whether to buy from you.

Practicing As You Play — The Value of Routine

In sports, coaches emphasize the benefits from "practicing as you play." Athletes play better when key performance attributes become routine. Basketball players practice free throws enough that they become routine, down to how many times they dribble the ball before shooting. With routine comes consistency and with consistency comes more points. *When simpler issues become routine, difficult issues become simpler.*

In music, teachers also emphasize the benefits from practicing as you play. For instance, in guitar playing, you benefit from practicing as you play so that when performing, fingering and chord patterns are not new—they are routine. With routine, the guitar player can apply more thought to what other musicians are playing, which allows them to insert tasteful improvisations during a performance. The accomplished guitar player does not need to think about routine play thus creating more capacity for improvisational play—the difference between good players and special players. *When simpler issues become routine, difficult issues become simpler.*

In sales, your productivity also benefits by practicing as you play. *The Five Abilities* teaches you to practice as you play by making routine the process of assessing and identifying customer problems, thus giving you increased capacity for innovative problem solving. Identifying the source of a problem, with five simple questions (e.g., *The Five Abilities*), gives you increased capacity for delivering special and unique value for your customers. *When simpler issues become routine, difficult issues become simpler.*

> *When simpler issues become routine, difficult issues become simpler.*

Repeat Business

In today's global economy, people who make buying decisions are more mobile than ever before. The days of the 30-year career with a single employer are history in most Western economies, and we see the signs that the same is happening in Asian and Latin American industries.

Millennials make up the largest portion of our workforce. In 2012, *Forbes* published an article[1] by Jeanne Meister, citing that those in this generation change jobs, on average, every 4.4 years. In 2016, we are well into the new "Gig Economy" where employees treat jobs as temporary projects—expecting and accepting that they will be looking for a new "gig" every 12-24 months. It's reminiscent of my days as a musician when we constantly hunted for new gigs because every job only lasted until we played our last song.

Winning new business remains important, but lifelong customers represent the repeat business that earns you consistently growing revenue and higher profits, simply because the cost of winning additional business from existing customers is much less than winning new prospects. An article by Colin

Shaw, published on LinkedIn titled, "*15 Statistics That Should Change the Business World – But Haven't*"[2] lists many reasons why loyal customers are much more profitable than new ones. Performing well enough to win repeat business is critical to having a lifetime of success with people and companies, whether you are a salesperson or a CEO.

When I discuss the need for lifelong customers with executives and salespeople, I often see reluctance in their eyes because they assume lifelong customers take much more work. The reality is that establishing a customer culture and executing on it consistently is actually easier than winning a single piece of business. Let me share how *The Five Abilities* came to be and how it will help you win more business with more lifelong customers.

Birth of a Sales Framework

The Five Abilities is a common sense, people-oriented sales framework that guides you to the *best next actions* that move you ahead on the path to winning more business with more lifelong customers. This is about best next actions.

I started my business-to-business (B2B) selling career over three decades ago and I have studied a number of sales programs, frameworks, and methodologies. While they all offer good learning, nothing was better than getting out there to sell and *The Five Abilities* centers on that belief. This book and my consulting framework are all about giving you quick, new ideas that help you implement your best next actions today.

My First Sales Job

My first sales job was when, as a musician, we had to hunt down and book gigs—that and pitching my demo tapes door-to-door in Hollywood. Next, I sold checks for American Bank Stationery, a great company, but we were so unknown in parts of my territory that I had to start many cold calls by proving we were a viable business.

These early sales experiences and the training I received were very valuable in helping me learn the fundamental challenges of delivering standard value propositions, trial closing, handling objections, and closing again. However, the best learning came from having to sell without a recognizable brand. Without a brand and the mindshare that comes with it, I had to learn how to prioritize market opportunities, fine-tune value propositions based on customer need, and quickly identify the personal motivations of decision-makers and influencers. I learned later in my career that these skills apply to all sales opportunities whether you sell for Rick's Red Ropes (my first entrepreneurial venture when I was eight years old), or strong brands such as Hewlett-Packard (HP) and Microsoft.

Internal Selling

At HP, *The Five Abilities* helped me to hone the important skill of internal selling. I had a global account sales territory, which required me to get help from people throughout the company. Working across multiple functions increased the importance of detailed but simple plans that enabled all stakeholders to provide optimal assistance to our sales efforts. We did a lot of planning, documenting, and presenting internally to other HP stakeholders in order to garner help, share best practices, and to get new ideas.

In the beginning, as with all of us, I was rough around the edges, to be kind to myself. I was the one asking all the questions after every training. The people at HP were always patient and knowledgeable. I learned a lot and after some successful years, I evolved from being the person asking all the questions to being one of the people fielding questions after planning and training sessions. The questions often started with, "What do I do now?" just like when I was starting out. We would spend three to five days of concentrated effort in offsite sessions and still people would come away asking, "What do I do now?"

We typically had a handle on our mission, goals, and strategies. We knew our products fairly well. We knew the key decision-makers, or at least their titles—but still, it often wasn't clear what to do next. The planning sessions resulted in neatly filled-out forms and very detailed analysis, but they didn't always point the way to the best next actions that helped us overcome typical sales obstacles such as strong incumbents, decision-makers who refused to meet with us, and the key influencers who were selling against us. At the time, I had no easy way to explain how I determined my own best next actions or how to help other salespeople to determine their *own* best next actions, so my coaching was less than optimal.

A Needed Nudge

Fast forward to 1990 when HP and Andersen Consulting (AC, now Accenture) won a very large, highly competitive manufacturing project at the Boeing Company. I was the salesperson leading the HP effort and the aerospace manufacturing industry was one of HP's target vertical markets. The contract with Boeing's subsidiary—Boeing Commercial Airplane Group—was HP's largest new business win in the aerospace manufacturing industry that year. As a result, we had requests from people in both HP and Andersen Consulting for a "win report."

We presented that report at an Andersen Consulting Partner's conference in Atlanta, Georgia, which led to more requests for our learnings from people across the HP sales community. Eventually, with encouragement from my local management, I got an invitation from our SVP of Global Accounts to present our win report to all of HP's global account sales leaders. He wanted me to show how others could advance their own opportunities and specifically to talk about what we did that everyone could learn and repeat.

I had just a week to prepare and I built a 30-page presentation detailing the specific things we did. I thought it was good, but my manager bluntly said, "Nobody's gonna care about all that. It's too specific to Boeing. You gotta make it simple and repeatable for everyone." The Global Accounts SVP, who had initiated the invitation, confirmed my manager's advice saying, "I just want seven or eight slides that people can remember. I want something *clever and catchy* that everyone can run with."

Clever and Catchy

Like all of us in sales, we know that presentations must be clear and concise. However, this early career experience taught me that what I see as short-and-sweet is often *not* what my audience considers concise.

When I practiced that 30-slide presentation, I was able to get through it in 45 minutes. Of course, that was with nobody asking questions, which is the last thing you should expect—or want.

The most important input was from my SVP: I needed to present something that was *clever and catchy*—relevant advice specific to our win, but also good general advice that everyone could apply to his or her own situation. If your audience does not get a few "gems" that stick in their minds, you have not done your job.

Like the "hook" in a hit song, you want the listener to hear something they cannot stop replaying in their head. In the case of a song, you want them compelled to sing it. In the case of selling products and services, you want them anxious to use it. Look for opportunities to create hits by making your points clever and catchy.

I was starting the presentation over and was out of time, so I met again with my AC partner, Mike. He said, "All I know is we made more sales calls than any project I've been involved in!" We met with over 200 Boeing executives and managers, many on multiple occasions, because we had to. Compared to the incumbent providers, HP and AC were relatively unknown so we needed to be more *visible* in the right way, at the right time, with the right people.

We also trailed behind the incumbents in credibility, because we lacked experience with this customer. We learned that testimonials were more valuable than standard presentations and that it was more *credible* for each of us to present the value proposition of the other partner, therefore becoming their testimonial, so we learned to present each other's products and services.

Adding to our challenge, Boeing had just gone through a failed deployment with a new factory-automation supplier so their executives were extremely hesitant to choose new suppliers over incumbents. To overcome this we built a demonstration that allowed customers to use our hardware and software in a simulated factory setting where they assembled model airplanes while using our hardware and software. We demonstrated to and educated the Boeing decision-makers how we were *viable* and *capable*. (*More on this later.*)

Finally, we made ourselves available anytime. All the decision-makers and influencers had our home phone numbers. (This was before mobile phones.) Boeing, like most successful companies, works 24/7 and when there are problems they don't care what time it is. We learned later that the evaluation team often could not reach our competitors in the evenings and it frustrated them that they had to wait until the next day to get answers. We were not only available, but oftentimes we were still at the customer site in the evening hours, and were able to meet in their offices. We had many late-night face-to-face meetings, where we left the building with our future customers, to find that our cars were the only ones left in their parking lot.

The time came for me to make my revised presentation in Cupertino, CA, where our Global Accounts Leadership was meeting—it was now only seven slides. I covered just five critical points:

- How we created maximum *visibility* with all decision-makers and influencers.
- How we enhanced our *credibility* by having AC promote the benefits of HP and HP promote the benefits of AC.

- How we convinced key decision-makers on the *viability* of our joint solution by showing our success history and demonstrating our software and hardware in a way that allowed them to operate our solution on their own.
- How we gave proof of our collective *capability* by introducing Boeing leaders to existing customers and experts who had similar personal motivations before buying from us.
- How we displayed *reliability* throughout the process by always being accessible and quick to respond to questions.

Questions and positive comments came after almost every bullet point that I presented, so it was a very interactive session. At the end, the group of senior managers applauded while the Senior Vice-President complimented me on being "clever and catchy." Interspersed in the applause were comments like "great," "very creative," and perhaps the highest compliment, "Can you come to Chicago and present to my team?" It was at that moment when I realized that I had developed a tool that could be helpful to others beyond just me.

On the flight home, I thought through my sales experiences to date, wondering if *The Five Abilities* applied universally to other successes in which I had participated or observed. Was sales success largely about being better than the competition at VISABILITY, CREDABILITY, VIABILITY, CAPABILITY, and RELIABILITY? Without exception the answer was, "Yes." Beyond that win, did *The Five Abilities* help me in winning lifelong customers at a more consistent rate? Did *The Five Abilities* help me to be a better teammate and coach to others? Yes, and yes.

Likewise, the salespeople I admired most found ways to be more *visible* in productive and professional ways. They were instantly *credible* because they were well informed, and they were great at communicating their knowledge. They had a nose for good and bad business so that they always spent their time on *viable* opportunities. They all took pains to understand how their win would be the customer's win and always tuned product presentations to show they were *capable* of delivering the win each individual decision-maker was looking for. They were *reliable* for everyone. Whether a customer or co-worker, they were always there to help.

Thus was born *The Five Abilities* **Sales Framework.**

Winning Lifelong Customers Using *The Five Abilities*®

The Five Abilities®

- VISABILITY* – Being seen in the right way by the right people at the right time
- CREDABILITY* – Showing superior knowledge about your industry and that of your customers
- VIABILITY – Verifying the needs and readiness of both the seller and buyer
- CAPABILITY – Delivering on the personal reasons people make business decisions
- RELIABILITY – Always being accountable *when* the unexpected happens

*Knowingly misspelled

To be clear, sticking to a simple framework like *The Five Abilities* does not make your job easy, but it does make you more consistent. That in itself serves as simplification for you, and it makes you more predictable to your customers, therefore making you easier to work with. It also makes it probable that you can consistently repeat successes, which is critical both in the world of selling and business in general.

Since 1990, I have honed *The Five Abilities* while using the principles to guide my teams in growing our business more than we might have otherwise. I've used it as a tool to resolve confusion when people asked, "Now what do we do?" I have used these principles to guide channel partners, and I am now sharing *The Five Abilities* sales framework to help others achieve the kinds of successes I've been blessed with throughout my career.

My Success History

In MBA school, on the first day of class, each professor would introduce himself or herself and ask if we had questions. Without fail, someone would ask about the professor's real-world experience. Most of our professors had real-world experiences but the few who did not had to work to gain credibility and acceptance with the students. It wasn't always a fair assessment of the professor but it was a need from students who wanted to learn from people who had done it before.

Well—I've done it before. I've had sales success in small Corporate America (American Bank Stationery or ABS), very large global corporations (HP and Microsoft), and in a few entrepreneurial ventures (Papa Aldo's Pizza Franchise and JacquiBob Music Productions). I've succeeded in all areas of the broad business category called sales:

- Cold-calling, telesales, and territory management—check
- Enterprise, global, and major account sales—check

- Entrepreneurial selling with no brand recognition—check
- Selling for a fire brand, market leader—check
- Selling for a fire brand, in decline—check
- Technical design wins and channel management—check
- Business development - Building the environment and infrastructure necessary for us to sell—check
- Convincing our kids to go to bed early on school nights—mostly check

At American Bank Stationery (ABS), I established the role of inside sales as a real sales role versus a role to on-ramp salespeople, as it was defined when I first took the job. I closed significant new business in a territory where all sales and support were by phone. I earned a promotion to a field role in half the time expected, and I made my quota numbers in each of the three years I was with American Bank Stationery, which included part-time work during my first quarter of MBA school. So even before I called it *The Five Abilities*, I was using it to sell checks.

In 1990, per the previous story, the effort that led to the formal creation of *The Five Abilities* resulted in the largest aerospace manufacturing win for HP in that fiscal year. In 1991, I won President's Club honors—a designation given each year to HP's top 100 salespeople, in a salesforce of 15,000 people. The winners must have at least three consecutive years of top results in the areas of sales, customer satisfaction, teamwork, and creativity. While at HP, I carried a quota for eight years and only missed my number once when everyone on the Boeing team missed due to a delayed new product shipment.

At Microsoft, I carried quota for fourteen of the eighteen years I was there. I was a manager or executive in all roles while at Microsoft. Of the fourteen quota-carrying years, teams that I managed won five Team of the Year awards, and we exceeded our overall revenue targets in all but one year. I started at Microsoft as a Marketing Manager and moved up through the ranks to Vice-President OEM Sales—Asia/Global

Device Partners, managing as many as 300 people across Asia and our Redmond, Washington, headquarters.

Through all those years in ABS, HP, and Microsoft, I was able to use and hone *The Five Abilities* to manage my own actions as well as those of my teams. I vetted the framework in real-world success experiences and observations of the successful people with whom I had the blessing to work. The framework has also benefitted our entrepreneurial ventures. With the Papa Aldo's Pizza franchise, we did a lot of work to increase our VISABILITY in the community and to enhance our VIABILITY as a great option for families on the go. I also started JacquiBob Music Productions to write, record, and sell children's music to raise a little money for local groups such as Seattle Children's Hospital and the local chapter of the YMCA. My selling actions led to reviews in *Billboard Magazine* and *USA Today*, along with many other newspapers and magazines. That publicity resulted in five of my original songs being on the radio in all 50 US states for eighteen months. The radio play got me invited to do a live radio show at Disneyland. All because I was able to pick up a phone and deliver a customer-focused value proposition to disc jockeys, record storeowners, and music reviewers.

I've done it before, just like you. I don't intend to brag but instead to answer the question that my MBA professors always got about what qualifies me to write and consult on this topic. I'm confident *The Five Abilities* will make you more productive just as it did for my teams and me.

How to Use This Book

Winning Lifelong Customers With The Five Abilities is a user's reference manual and a short read. Sales, like sports and music, is not something in which you learn just by reading about it. Therefore, I offer brief, real-life examples of how *The Five Abilities* have helped me, along with the people I have worked with. The examples will spark ideas and excitement such that you cannot wait to see your next customers so that you can tune your skill by doing your job.

DO THE EXERCISES. The exercises at the end of each chapter are tools that will propel you into immediate action. Take the ten minutes to do them and come back to them when problems arise, so that they become habit. These are habits I employ and have trained others to use. You will recognize them as challenges you face each day.

You can read the entire book or turn right to the answers that address specific challenges. My goal is to make you excited to get back in front of customers or clients with new ideas about why they should buy from you and why they should be your lifelong customers.

(Note: If you do happen to read the book cover-to-cover first, thank you. Second, you will see important phrases that are important to know and put in practice, no matter what part of the book you read. For instance, you will read about the suspicion-of-value and the 30-second value proposition throughout the book. This is to ensure comprehension and clarity even if you do not read the book cover-to-cover.)

Here are a few questions to help you decide the best way to use this book:

- *Are decision-makers and influencers asking to meet with you?* If the answer is "No," start with Chapter 2, which describes how to earn the right VISABILITY with prospective and existing customers. Even if you've met with the customer, if they are not proactively reaching out to meet with you again, you have not earned the right VISABILITY.
- *Are decision-makers and influencers asking you for advice beyond what your product or service delivers?* If the answer is "No," Chapter 3 on how to earn CREDABILITY will help you learn the best next steps on which you can act. When customers ask for advice, rather than

just product information, it means they see you as an advisor. This is where you need to be in order to have the CREDABILITY necessary to win lifelong customers.

- *Are discussions with customers primarily about results and not on costs?* If cost or price is the dominant concern for your customer, you might need to reassess whether the opportunity represents the VIABILITY both you and your customer wants in a business opportunity. You can learn how to earn and recognize VIABILITY in Chapter 4.

- *Are you clear on the personal buying motivations for both decision-makers and influencers?* If you do not yet know what is driving the people who are influencing the purchase decision, you will gain much insight from Chapter 5 on the CAPABILITY of helping customers satisfy their personal motivations for buying. People make business decisions for personal reasons and you must satisfy those personal motivations in order to win lifelong customers.

- *Are decision-makers and influencers still asking, "What happens when something goes wrong?"* If they are, then it might be most important for you to learn how to earn RELIABILITY, which is the subject of Chapter 6. Lifelong customers do not ask, because they just know that you will take care of them.

In Chapter 7 on Scratch-Pad Planning, you will find *The Five Abilities Action Matrix* that allows you to assess, in an instant, where you are on the way to winning a sale and to identify the best next actions needed to move forward in the process.

In Chapter 8, I emphasize the importance of finding and hiring people who are motivated to sell for the right reasons. You will use this learning along with *The Five Abilities* to build a customer-winning culture. A customer culture applies not only to the companies you are selling to, but to the people who make the decisions within your own company. It is important to advocate for your customer without taking sides against your own company—something referred to as "going native." Going native refers to when the salesperson is more interested in getting what their customers want than in doing the right thing for the company they sell for. This leads to overcommitting and under-delivering. The best salespeople never go native, but others still see them in that way. You need to eliminate that perception in order to garner the help you need from peers and partners.

In Chapter 9, I discuss the changes to the sales profession brought upon by digital communications and social media. While this book specifically focuses on the ever-important personal engagement side of selling, I feel it is important that my readers and everyone learn that none of today's technologies have replaced the desire by decision-makers to know that they are buying from a human being who is looking out for their well-being.

In Chapter 10, I summarize the concepts in this book and share a short anecdote about the best sale I have ever made.

In Summary

You are most productive when you build quick, credible plans that drive immediate actions, which allows you to spend more time engaging with customers in thoughtful ways. The more we engage with our customers and prospects, in meaningful ways, the more we understand what motivates them to buy. With the knowledge of what motivates decision-makers and influencers, we can continually tune our plans and actions so that we can enhance our customer's results—thus increasing our probability of winning a sale and a lifelong customer.

My goal in writing this book is to make it easier for you and your sales teams to wake up each morning better able to identify your best next actions on the way to winning a sale. It is not about slick hard closes because that does not win you lifelong customers. This book will guide you to see that customers look for five common-sense abilities when deciding whether to buy from you or your competitor. With *The Five Abilities*, you will find your best next actions on the way to winning lifelong customers—the lifeblood of enterprise selling.

Let's go!

CHAPTER 2
VISABILITY
SEEN IN THE RIGHT WAY,
BY THE RIGHT PEOPLE, AT THE RIGHT TIME

In this chapter, you will learn how to build a value proposition based on a clear definition of what the customer needs that you are selling. You will learn how to create value propositions that stem from customer need enough that they want to learn more by engaging with you.

You will learn how to build a 30-second value proposition in the customer's terms—because if you cannot state the value a customer gets in less than 30 seconds, you are probably short on value. You will learn how to have a 3-minute conversation, which follows a customer showing interest in your proposition. You will learn how to build a 30-minute presentation based on the value in which the customer showed interest versus the presumptive sales pitch on which too many still rely. Lastly, you will learn how to tweet your propositions.

Creating a Suspicion-of-Value

When the customer suspects you have value to offer, such that they want to learn more, you have created the VISABILITY necessary to ignite and advance a productive sales engagement. I call this creating a *suspicion-of-value* that causes decision-makers and influencers to want to learn more from you. How do you know when you have created an effective suspicion-of-value?

Are decision-makers and their influencers asking to meet with you because they have a suspicion-of-value about you, your company, and your product?

A simple question with a simple answer that tells you a lot. If the customer is pursuing you proactively, you have created a suspicion-of-value that is compelling them to invest their valuable time to learn more. When customers ask to learn more you have advanced the opportunity from a cold prospect to a warm lead. On the other hand, when you are the constant pursuer it indicates that you have not delivered enough of the right information to create a compelling suspicion-of-value in the mind of the customer.

(Note: A very visible brand or a highly credible reference may get you a first meeting, but you never get the second meeting without the customer at least suspecting strong value in what you offer. Being able to create a suspicion-of-value is necessary no matter how you get that first meeting.)

Build and Deliver a 30-3-30-3 to Earn VISABILITY

30-Second Value Proposition:

If you cannot get the customer interested in less than 30 seconds, you are not expressing value that addresses their need.

- Goal: Earn a meeting by progressing from sales pitch to sales engagement.
- Strategy: Create a *suspicion of value* in the customer's mind so that they ask to know more.

3-Minute Conversation:

- Goal: Earn the opportunity to have a formal discussion with decision-makers about your offering.
- Strategy: Give the customer compelling information that confirms their original suspicion-of-value.

30-Minute Presentation for Meeting with Customer:

- Goal: Minimum acceptable – Get a second meeting / Maximum acceptable – Win the business.
- Strategy: Present information that convinces the customer that you can create valuable outcomes for them.

3-Second Tweet:

If you cannot get the customer to click through in 140 characters or less, you are not expressing value in their terms.

- Goal: Reader clicks through.
- Strategy: Create a *suspicion of value* in the customer's mind so that they want to click through.

Building and Delivering a 30-Second Value Proposition

I have lost count of the number of times sales and marketing people have said to me, "There's no way I can fit all our value into a 30-second statement." However, when we break down what a value proposition really is, the purpose of a 30-second value proposition becomes clear.

A value proposition is simply a proposal or suggestion for the customer to consider. It is not an absolute and it is not a close. It is a suggestion that there is value in what you have to offer and that your customer would benefit from evaluating it. The goal of the 30-second value proposition is to start the sales engagement by creating enough suspicion-of-value in the mind of the decision-maker, such that they ask to learn more from you. When prospects ask to learn more, you have evolved from a one-way sales pitch to a two-way business engagement—right where you want to be. You have evolved to the point where the customer is ready to help you understand the value they need from your offering.

This is a take on the age-old elevator pitch. A very brief, compelling, and memorable statement should you happen to be fortunate enough to have a few seconds (e.g., riding an elevator) with an important person. It is a tool to keep us from wasting the moment and to give us an opening sentence in case we get nervous. Optimally, we want this lucky situation to result in the person asking us to get out of the elevator to continue the conversation. This can only happen if you create a suspicion-of-value. The 30-second value proposition is simply a structured way to build your elevator pitch.

An Elevator Pitch That Worked

One of my many Microsoft roles was managing the sales relationship with one of our largest, most well-known customers, a major player in the technology industry. We had a global team managing a multi-billion dollar sales quota, which included what Microsoft called "design wins"—convincing companies to design devices such as PCs, phones, servers, and even gas pumps, optimized for our software.

I was three months into the role and we had scheduled a meeting at the annual Consumer Electronics Show (CES) to discuss the merits of building mobile devices on the Windows platform. In attendance would be executives from both companies and their celebrity CEO, who I will refer to as Marcus. He was still very involved with the business and doing many interviews for business publications.

I worked closely with Laura, who managed the overall relationship with Microsoft and while she did not have a sales quota, she won when Microsoft did well, just as I won when her company did well. We had a strong win-win partnership.

Laura and I arrived at the conference room forty-five minutes early to make sure everything was prepared properly. We tidied the room and put information packets in front of each chair. We finished and sat in the waiting area, when in walked Marcus. He was alone and fifteen minutes early.

Laura introduced us, and then left to find the rest of their executives. I called our executives to get an ETA and with about ten minutes to go I found myself sitting in what felt like an elevator with Marcus, whose picture just happened to be on the cover of *Fortune* magazine, a copy of which was on the table in front of us. Out of habit, from my training at HP, I had prepared my 30-second value proposition that I hoped would result in Marcus asking for more information.

Marcus was aware that I was new in the role, so he politely opened the conversation asking how I liked working with his people. We had about a minute of small talk and then I said, "Marcus, Laura and I were just in China and I think we might need to rethink how you're going to sell your products there." I knew that China was of great interest to Marcus and thought this would create a suspicion-of-value in his mind. He got a look of curiosity on his face and asked, "What's the problem?" I responded, "Most Chinese consumers don't have credit cards or Internet access so they can't buy over the phone or online." That led to a series of questions from him and overall, a great conversation. It ended (or so I thought) when the other executives arrived.

(Note: This was in 2001 when most Chinese consumers still did not have credit cards. They had to pay by cash or money order to complete the purchase with retailers. The massive modernization in China has made this a moot point, but it was a very real problem for many companies in 2001.)

We sat down to start the meeting and while everyone was making introductions, I updated Laura on what had transpired. After the introductions, much to my surprise, Marcus said to the group, "Rick and I weren't quite finished with our conversation yet." He turned to ask me for suggestions, we talked for another couple of minutes, and then he asked both Laura and I for quarterly updates on China and whatever else was not going well with our joint projects.

Those updates turned into discussions that extended beyond China. I ended up having those quarterly updates with Marcus for two and a half years, and I continued to get his family holiday cards three years after moving to another role. It all started with a 30-second value proposition that created a suspicion-of-value in his mind that we could provide help.

Once you understand that your goal in that initial exchange is to create a suspicion-of-value and not to presume you have the answer, it's much easier to create a 30-second value proposition that sparks interest. You quickly learn that you do not have to become a fast-talker, like at the end of television drug commercials, and communicate all of your features and benefits. Whether you are selling for a big brand name or an unknown start-up, once you have created a suspicion-of-value in the mind of the customer, you have advanced from a sales pitch to a business exchange—right where you need to be.

How Do We Build Effective 30-Second Value Propositions?

An effective 30-second value proposition shows some understanding of the customer's challenges, a deep knowledge of your products and services, and ends with a comment or question that compels the customer to ask for more information. You combine information about the industry, the customer, and your offerings to build a statement that will spark interest.

Product managers are experts on their products. Marketing managers typically have deep knowledge of the products and the industry. The salesperson should be knowledgeable on both—but it's most important that you are the expert on your customer. You cannot design or deliver an effective value proposition without detailed knowledge of the customer's business and the problems they need to solve. Your opening discussion needs to show you as conversant, but more importantly, curious about the customer's needs. Through the process of getting to know decision-makers, you will be able to hone your value proposition so that it's stated in the customer's terms.

(Note: In some companies, salespeople are required to present standard content to customers no matter what. The intent is good in that product teams want to avoid committing to things the company cannot actually do. However, without exception, the most successful salespeople develop content that is specific to the customer's needs, without misrepresenting the products, services, and companies they represent. It is never in their interest to break a promise to a customer. My advice to product and marketing managers is that if you trust your salespeople they will produce for you.)

Steps to building an effective 30-second value proposition:

- **Step 1:** List industry/business changes, challenges, and issues that you know your customer has. You learn these by reading general news, following social media relevant to the customer's industry, and reading the few trade rags that are still in circulation.
  Example: Competition is increasing in the commercial airplane industry. Innovations come out at an ever-accelerating pace making it harder to compete.
- **Step 2:** List the problems created for the customer/client based on the challenges and issues you listed.
  Example: Airplane manufacturers must continually reduce time-to-market with innovations and improvements to

motivate commercial airline executives to modernize their fleets.

- **Step 3:** Identify solutions you provide that address the customer/client's problems.
  Example: Our CAD (computer-aided-design) software reduces airplane design and test cycles by fifty percent and eliminates the need for mock-ups—cutting cost significantly.
- **Step 4:** Suspicion-of-value you want to create. What question(s) do you want the customer to ask?
  Example: How will we do airplane walk-throughs with customers? How will we retrain our design engineers? How will we design manufacturing tools?
- **Step 5:** Write one to three versions of your 30-second value proposition. The purpose of writing multiples is to help you learn them without reading them. You want your value propositions to be conversational and not scripted. It is also helpful to have a repertoire of value propositions so you can adjust for the customer situation, which helps you be more conversational.
  Example: The speed of innovation is making it harder to compete for new airline business. Long periods between product launches can be a competitive disadvantage. Our new CAD software reduces airplane design and test cycles by as much as fifty percent. Would this help you be more competitive?

(Note: This is a real 30-second value proposition that was successful for one of HP's strongest competitors in the engineering workstation business. It led to a strong suspicion-of-value and the engagement resulted in years of business and millions of dollars in revenue at Boeing.)

Preparing for Your 3-Minute Conversation

When you have done enough to create a suspicion-of-value in the mind of the customer such that they ask to know more, you must be able to answer in a way that either earns you a formal meeting or gets you introduced to relevant decision-makers or influencers. To accomplish this, it's important to anticipate the questions and to have additional information ready that compels the customer to want a meeting with you.

To get to a formal meeting you must create a sense of urgency around the potential loss should they not make a decision about the benefits you offer. Some of the best practices I have seen come from companies that sell airplanes and smartphone components.

Selling Airplanes at Boeing

At Boeing, their salespeople know—off the top of their heads—the average fuel cost savings and payback periods that airlines can achieve by replacing outdated airplanes. In the early days of the 757 and 767 airplanes, Boeing salespeople could recite cost savings from having two people in the cockpit versus the three that were required in earlier generation airplanes. There was always an opportunity cost for holding off learning about innovations.

Boeing salespeople could advise airline executives about which new routes to add with estimates on the additional profit for each route. The salespeople had analysis on the best locations for hubs and the best places to store spare parts. Boeing salespeople are among the best examples of trusted advisors—in less than three minutes, they can validate the suspicion-of-value about new profits or cost reductions, and show the customer why they will benefit by learning more.

Selling Smartphone Components

In the smartphone industry, two components dramatically affect the usability of the device: the quality of the glass and the touch sensors. These two components contribute greatly to user satisfaction. With each successive innovation cycle, touch and typing becomes more accurate—glass gets thinner, lighter, and more durable—the phones just work better.

Glass manufacturers such as Corning, Samsung, and LGE employ salespeople who can quickly describe the benefits of new-generation glass and the opportunity cost of not making a decision to incorporate the new component. In two to three minutes, they can forecast an estimated reduction in phone sales without the new technology. They talk about lower customer satisfaction when other device manufacturers bring out their new-generation phones. They also talk about increased support costs. They discuss their company's limited production capacity for building the new-generation glass, thus creating the sense of urgency to decide, which leads to the need for a formal discussion.

In both the Boeing and smartphone situations, salespeople use the 3-minute conversation to describe the opportunity costs in a way that presents them as advisors and not simply as salespeople looking for an order. They also create a sense of urgency that is a best friend to salespeople. When you use the 3-minute conversation to open minds on the advice you offer, you are more likely to open doors of decision-makers and influencers who will someday be lifelong customers.

Constructing the 30-Minute Presentation

The fastest way to waste the opportunity of a face-to-face meeting with a customer is to present *all* of your canned features and benefits before you understand their priorities. Unfortunately, it is all too common, especially with large companies, for sales and marketing people to assume that every customer needs everything they sell. Moreover, even if that were true, it would not mean that every bit of your offering addresses their current priorities. Instead, the foundational elements of the presentation must show that you can make true the proposition that sparked the customer's interest in the first place—what they deem to be valuable.

This process is the reverse of the way most product and marketing teams build their presentations because it is their job to include all the features and benefits of their products. They include all the information they think will be useful to the customer and build a story around it. This is understandable because, again, they are the product experts, not the individual customer experts. It is the job of the salesperson to be the individual customer expert so that decision-makers see information specific to their most urgent needs.

Start with what caused the customer to have a suspicion-of-value in the first place, confirm through the 3-minute conversation that you have it right, and use the presentation to show how you can get it done.

In the Marcus example, we worked with Laura and her team to create a joint plan for how we could go to market in China with a traditional channel model while also keeping the build-to-order value of that company's product offerings.

In the airplane example, the majority of the presentation would cover all the things we'd have to do in order for the digital walk-through to become real, since that was where they would realize the most reduced costs and accelerated time to market, the customer's priority concerns.

The 3-Second Value Proposition — a Tweet

A tweet is an abbreviated version of the 30-second value proposition. In today's digital marketing/social media world, it is a requirement that you be even more concise with your value statements because you must create that suspicion-of-value in 140 characters or less. You need to create enough curiosity that they want to learn more by clicking through, contacting you, or by viewing your various forms of digital content.

In the airplane example, such a tweet is simple: "You can reduce airplane design costs by 50%. See more." In addition, of course, a relevant picture would help.

What Is the Wrong VISABILITY?

All VISABILITY is not good visibility. The wrong visibility is what many view as the stereotypical salesperson—a schmoozer. Charming, extroverted, attractive, aggressive, and ... annoying.

Schmoozers want to have lunch and drinks and call that a relationship. Schmoozers pitch their products during a kid's soccer game. Schmoozers stop the customer on the sidewalk and act like a best friend, even when they've only met the customer once at a conference. On the other hand, schmoozers waste social time with a customer talking only about business, leaving the customer with the sense that the schmoozer only has the capacity to have a transactional exchange. Who wants that? Nobody.

Annoying salespeople are those who ask for meetings with no new value to offer. They have one play in their book, which is to present their content whether it is relevant to the customer or not. In addition, they have only one goal for every meeting: ask for the business. "Close hard and close often" is their mantra.

People who advocate this behavior often refer to sales as just a numbers game. Quantity of calls rules over quality. While this approach may work for transactional sales, it is not appropriate or effective for enterprise sales. The actual numbers game is really all about how many influential people you know who will pick up the phone any time you call. It is about the number of people who want to talk with you because of the value they suspect you have. Annoying salespeople do not earn a place in the decision-maker's Rolodex, which means that they cannot play the numbers game even if it were effective.

What Is the Right VISABILITY?

The right VISABILITY is when you are seen as a colleague delivering value with each interaction whether a sale is transacted or not. Having the right VISABILITY results in the relationship being as important as the benefits that ensue from whatever you sell. Great salespeople add value in each interaction by asking questions that cause the customer to think in new and different ways. In turn, the customers' answers help you understand their business and personal motivations so that your proposals are more precise and have a higher likelihood of benefiting both the buyer and the seller.

Winning lifelong customers requires that we show up in ways that make prospective customers value and enjoy time with us. The baseline is that you are a pleasant, engaging, and good human being, but these are just *minimum* requirements. Lifelong customers buy from you because the value of the relationship is as important as the product or service you deliver.

The Right Time to Earn VISABILITY Is When the Customer Is Not Buying

You benefit greatly when the customer views you as the best *before* the competition begins. At minimum, the customer must view you in a favorable light when it comes time for them to begin their investigation and evaluation. This is why the right time to earn **VISABILITY** is before the customer starts the buying process.

Winter Olympic sports are instructive in learning the concept of the right **VISABILITY**. Some winter sports offer clear winners and losers, such as downhill skiing and bobsledding, where it is simply about who goes the fastest. Conversely, there are sports like freestyle skiing and figure skating where there is a combination of technical requirements and artistic elements. Human beings score the artistic element on subjective personal observations, just as business people do when making buying decisions.

Athletes will tell you that any sport scored on subjective personal observation is impacted by the judges' perceptions before the competition starts. If an athlete enters the competition ranked as the best in the sport, the judges will look for that best performance and often will see it even if it doesn't happen.

The same is true in selling. The sales and marketing teams that the customer pre-judges as the best have the advantage when the competition starts. In the pre-buying stages of customer interaction, you are simply competing for mindshare, expecting that someday in the future they will need the help available from your products or services. You are competing to become the most knowledgeable and trusted of the potential competitors so that when it comes time for the customer to evaluate and decide, they already expect the best from you.

Relating When the Customer is Not Buying

You do this by finding ways to relate to the customer in human ways. You also find ways to help decision-makers and influencers, in real ways, before they become paying customers. Any effort to develop a deep relationship in the midst of a competition encounters skepticism. People are people and when they know they are being pitched they will be guarded.

If, on the other hand, you put in the genuine effort to develop a relationship with the customer when they are not buying, they have the capacity to view you with a more open mind. This is particularly important in Asian and Latin American cultures where having an existing relationship is a clear prerequisite before any real selling can occur. The same is largely true for American and European cultures even though the prerequisite is not as overt. Personal trust is what decision-makers want from those with whom they do business. Building that trust is harder in the middle of a sales cycle because the only certainty is that the salesperson wants the customer's money.

Relationship Building or Schmoozing?

This part of the sales relationship—relating when the customer is not buying—is the most misunderstood part of selling because many consider it stereotypical behavior: meaningless schmoozing. What changes it from schmoozing to relating is when you simply use the time to get to know and help someone so that you can relate on a personal level. Once you have removed the barriers you are able to learn how you best help the decision-maker who is ready to share their needs with you and—as you must remember—makes business decisions for personal reasons.

Dinner with the CIO of Boeing

When I was at HP, we hosted an Open Systems conference at Cambridge Technology Group in Boston, Massachusetts. One of my guests was then the CIO of Boeing, who I will refer to as Terrill. We ended the first day with dinner at The Boston Museum of Fine Arts. The evening started with wine and a 30-minute tour of the museum, in which we accompanied our customers. Following the tour, we sat down to dinner, where I sat to Terrill's left.

On Terrill's right, another salesperson went into pitch mode with his customer from the minute we sat down. The salesperson had printed slides and was doing a full-blown presentation right there at the dinner table. Anyone could tell that his customer was not comfortable and it made Terrill uncomfortable because, as he told me later, he thought the same thing was going to happen to him.

I tapped Terrill's arm and asked, "What do you like doing when you're not working?" Terrill smiled and started talking about his love of hiking and travel. The dinner lasted ninety minutes and we spent almost the whole time talking about where we liked to hike and travel. We had big laughs about mistakes we had made while backpacking. We did spend ten minutes talking about Open Systems, and how it could help Boeing, but we found a way to fit it naturally into the discussion without me presenting anything.

At the end of the dinner, we were supposed to send our customers off to tour the museum by themselves, a time for them to enjoy the museum without a salesperson tagging along. We got up from the table and Terrill shook my hand saying, "Thank you for not doing to me what that guy did to his customer." He then invited me to tour the museum with him so we could continue our conversation. We had a great conversation and we both gave each other recommendations on great hikes in the Pacific Northwest of the United States.

Of course, some would call this schmoozing, but if you asked Terrill, he would say it was a genuine conversation. Incredibly successful salespeople do not schmooze—they relate. From that evening on, I was always able to get time with Terrill when necessary. He would also occasionally reach out to me even after I left HP, when I was no longer selling to Boeing.

Helping Before the Customer Starts Buying

Only providing help when the buying process starts is the worst thing a salesperson can do. Customers evaluate your offers of help differently when they are in the midst of a buying decision. They know you are competing and naturally apply more scrutiny to what they hear or see even if you are genuinely offering help.

When you consistently show a pattern of helping even when the customer is not in the process of making a purchase decision, the customer sees your offer of help as genuine outreach. Providing assistance and/or relevant information on a consistent and predictable basis earns you VISABILITY, CREDABILITY, and RELIABILITY, giving you an advantage when the competition starts because the customer has already learned to view you as an advisor.

One of my managers at Microsoft, Steven, had a wealth of experience and knowledge from years of success working in various product management, marketing, and field roles. He had a lot of market knowledge and customers considered him a SME in many areas of the IT industry. He also had a lot of influence when it came to getting things done inside of Microsoft. His VISABILITY and CREDABILITY as a SME put him in demand by our customers. Senior executives from all of our customers wanted to meet with Steven because they often felt they got more value from him than from leaders higher in the organization. Steven became part of the benefit of buying from

Microsoft. As a SME on so many topics, and as a customer-centric leader, Steven was a trusted advisor and a key part of our value proposition. To many customer executives, Steven's expertise was more valuable than our products and services. He was often a key reason customers continued to buy from us.

How Do You Help a Customer Who Has Not Asked for Help?

Customers have problems to solve whether they are in a buying mode or not. The fact that you have a company on your prospect list should mean that they have, or will have, a problem that your product or service can solve.

If you do just a little homework on your customer's industry, it's not hard to find information that could be helpful, or at minimum, show that you have relevant knowledge. It is important to remember that the goal is not to WOW them with information that only you have, even though it's nice when that happens. The goal is to help them with your knowledge about their issues. Customers want trusted advisors who can forecast where trouble will arise, rather than sellers who are waiting for a problem on which they can pounce.

For many years, I worked with a wonderful salesperson named Jennifer, and she was a natural helper. She had a prospective customer with whom she had an introductory meeting, during which time she learned that the key decision-maker had a family reunion coming up and that he had the responsibility for choosing the venue. Unfortunately, because he was so busy at work, he had no time to research locations.

Jennifer sent an email to a friend who was an event planner at a Seattle hotel to ask if she could offer suggestions. Long story short: Jennifer's prospective customer chose her friend's hotel and he could not thank her enough for seeing that he needed help and being proactive in getting it for him. One of the many wonderful traits possessed by Jennifer is that this joy in serving others is part of her being, so to her this had nothing to do with selling. This was simply her helping someone who needed it. No surprise that the decision-maker pre-judged her as the best when it came time for him to make a purchase decision. Not surprisingly, Jennifer is one of the most successful salespeople I know.

Caveat: If your help does not come from a place of genuine interest, customers will see that. This unfortunate circumstance is most apparent when the seller asks for recognition or special consideration after delivering help. My dad used to say, "If you have to ask for recognition, you don't deserve it." I have found his wisdom to be right in most cases.

If you are not visible before the buying process starts, you are too late. If you are just starting to learn the customer's language, processes, and problems when the decision-maker is already evaluating, you are aimlessly pitching when you should instead be delivering targeted advice. You might be thinking, "What if all the competitors are showing up late?" That might mean you are not behind, but it also means you are trying to sell to a customer who is nobody's priority, which is a problem in and of itself.

Cold Calls: Productive or Passé?

This topic comes up in almost all of my workshops. There are so many ways to be visible to customers in the digital age: websites, Twitter, Facebook, LinkedIn, Pinterest, Instagram, YouTube, webinars, text, WhatsApp, Snapchat, etc. Pick just about any letter in the alphabet and you can match it to a social media tool that promises to make you more visible to potential or existing customers and clients.

Additionally, the hot topic of advocacy has led many business leaders to believe that selling via references, which eliminates the need for cold calling, is the only way to get new business. With all this, some will tell you that the cold call is passé. I would tell you that cold calls are executed differently now versus fifteen years ago, but nonetheless they are a tool that successful salespeople use frequently because they work.

A cold call is simply a personable, productive outreach to another human being who has not yet met you. By personable

I mean outreach in person, by voice, and often by handwritten notes, which are returning to prominence. Email, LinkedIn Messaging, text, Twitter, etc., are not effective ways to connect unless you are already visible through other means, thus making these tools ineffective for cold calling. This brings up the topic of social media.

Why You Need Social Media Presence to Earn VISABILITY

There are many blogs and books from experts on social media. These few sentences will focus on why you need a good social media presence, in regards to modern selling. I will leave the "how to" advice to the experts.

Customers now expect that they can learn a great deal about you and your company before ever agreeing to meet with you. Having a fully filled out LinkedIn profile, an active Twitter account, a Facebook page, and a website are the low bar for entry in today's world of selling. The more popular social media tools are so commonplace that I often recommend that salespeople consider blogging, especially if they have knowledge that presents them as a SME. This can work even when the blog does not apply directly to their industry but, instead, makes a person more relatable.

I have a client who works in the technology industry but who decided to write a blog on her experiences as a Millennial settling into the early days of her independent life. She spent a few months working in New York City and wrote about simple, lighthearted things like finding an apartment, finding a good cup of coffee, and figuring out the transit system. Ultimately, she decided that NYC was not for her and because her job allowed her to live anywhere, she moved back to where she grew up, Seattle. Just for fun, she wrote more lighthearted blogs about the differences between NYC and Seattle.

After a year living in downtown Seattle, she wrote a short blog on how Millennials are utilizing mobile apps to get everything from transportation to freshly cooked meals—anywhere, anytime. She expounded on her generation's willingness to spend more to own less. A much simpler lifestyle than the house, two kids, and two-car garage that her parents' generation wanted. Not quite minimalist living because they consume a lot, but without the house, cars, and kids, they are more mobile and more adaptable to life changes that can happen when one finds a job opportunity, say in Singapore.

My client's blogs suddenly started being shared and tweeted by nationally known bloggers and suddenly my client had her fifteen minutes of fame, and more importantly, much broader visibility to a new community of peers. Her added VISABILITY resulted in getting interviews with companies that had rejected her before and now she is starting her climb up the ladder at a major online global retailer.

Certainly, she had to be credible, which I will talk about in the next chapter, but her customers (e.g., hiring managers) knew her before she ever met them. Social media is a way to connect with a prospective customer before you pursue that first personal outreach. With good social media presence, your first personal meeting is, in effect, no longer a first meeting.

In Summary

The most important part of creating VISABILITY starts long before you have your first conversation with a prospective customer. At the most basic level, you use the many sources of information available to learn about current challenges in your customer's industry, discover the effects of ongoing change, build a value proposition that resonates with decision-makers, and present your knowledge in ways and places where customers will discover you. You deliver your value propositions through various avenues from social media to direct interaction, keeping in mind that your goal is always to make a personal connection.

Using the latest "big data" tools, companies like Amazon are able to analyze our actions and behaviors in such detail that they are able to present us with buying opportunities without making that personal connection. This depth of knowledge has changed the way we shop and buy as individuals and it is starting to change the way companies make smaller transactional purchases. However, for large strategic investments, decision-makers still want a human being they trust—you—to be looking out for their personal best interests when formulating proposals.

For example, in the late 1980s, Electronic Data Interchange (EDI) was the hot technology that promised to reduce costs and reduce the amount of time decision-makers would have to spend with salespeople. EDI made data exchange much more efficient and because of the standards associated with data formatting and transmission, it meant that buying decisions would hinge purely on factual data exchange rather than the often charismatic and convincing promises made by a salesperson. That did not happen. We learned that when human decision-makers make big investments, they still act as people. In the words of a Senior Manager at Boeing, "We chose the people we wanted to work with."

Technology innovations may someday change this dynamic, but I doubt it. For now, we focus on **VISABILITY**, so that we can earn the right to have a lifelong relationship with the people who make those multi-million-dollar decisions. This is your first step to winning lifelong customers.

Putting It to Work: Exercises

(Note: I strongly suggest you take the time to apply these exercises to real issues you have now. By taking the time now, you will immediately address a hindrance to your sales productivity today, and you will start making *The Five Abilities* a habit rather than simple advice. Take ten minutes now. You'll be happy you did.)

VISABILITY – *To be seen in the right way, by the right people, at the right time*

Are decision-makers and their influencers asking to meet with you because they have a suspicion-of-value about you, your company, and your product?   Yes   No

If no:

Do you understand the decision-making process?   Yes   No

Do the decision-makers and the people who influence them understand what your products/services do, what they replace or rectify, and with whom they compete?   Yes   No

Do decision-makers and influencers suspect that you, your company, and your products/services have value for them? (Suspicion-of-Value)   Yes   No

For each no, document why you think this is happening.

1.

2.

3.

For each reason why the answer is no, document your best next action for changing it to yes.

1.

2.

3.

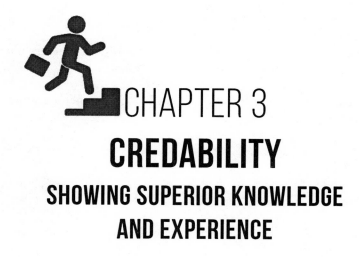

CHAPTER 3
CREDABILITY
SHOWING SUPERIOR KNOWLEDGE AND EXPERIENCE

The key principle for earning CREDABILITY is to prove that you can make your value proposition, as acknowledged by the customer, come true. You must understand and confirm what value the customer expects from you and show them how you will deliver it. You earn CREDABILITY by showing that your experience and expertise allows you to deliver on the value that made the customer interested enough to engage in the first place.

Are decision-makers and influencers asking you for advice beyond what your product/service delivers? When you can answer with a consistent, "Yes," you have earned the CREDABILITY needed to win business and win lifelong customers, because you have graduated from seller to advisor.

Actions That Earn CREDABILITY

Demonstrate how your product or service works and/or how you have done it before in ways that are relevant to the customer.

- Goal: Prove that you can make your value proposition happen.
- Strategy: Allow the customer to see your offering successfully used in a related environment and situation.

Educate your customers to help them be better, whether or not they are yet your customers.

- Goal: The customer sees you as a Subject Matter Expert (SME).
- Strategy: Introduce them to SMEs or educational opportunities associated with your offering.

Advocate for partners and peers who can offer help to your customers and clients.

- Goal: The customer sees you as a consultant and collaborator.
- Strategy: Show the customer that a long-term relationship is important to you even if you do not make a sale today.

Demonstrate

There are two main ways to facilitate demonstrations: (1) Live demonstrations, which are at a site, where your product or service is actually in operation. (2) Simulation demonstrations, where you must use a laboratory-type of environment for products that are brand new or when live options are not available because of competitive issues, geographic challenges, or simply timing requirements. Both are successful when done properly.

Live Demonstrations

The ultimate combination of demonstration and recommendation happens when you have the opportunity to show prospective customers a live site where existing customers are succeeding with your products and/or services. This is a powerful tool and if it's available to you, use it.

When I was selling manufacturing solutions, it was very common for us to invite prospective customers to visit another non-competitor customer site. For instance, in Seattle we hosted representatives from the Space Shuttle program who wanted to see how Boeing's Manufacturing Resource Planning (MRP) system worked on our proprietary operating system. It is always powerful for a prospect to hear from both you and your satisfied customer(s).

If you have this tool available, there are a few key things to ensure success when employing it:

- **Peer-to-peer exchanges are best.** When prospective customers visit a live site to see your products working, they also expect to talk with the host company's employees. They ask relevant questions about how your product has helped and want answers from someone who they see as a SME—other than you. For instance, if we bring a manufacturing executive to see our products they may not get the answers they need from an IT manager versus another manufacturing expert. A CFO might not get what they need from a bookkeeper or staff accountant.

- **Never over-script your customer who is sharing their experience.** Prospective customers want to hear what is really happening. Decision-makers understand that product and service implementations are never perfect. They want to see products working, but also want to know about challenges. When customers do not hear about hiccups they get suspicious, which loses you credibility rather than earning it. In addition, the customer who offers to demonstrate is giving up their time, and requiring them to spend an inordinate amount of time preparing is overly burdensome. We are always better off when customers have open, unscripted dialogue with their peers.

- **Do not let either customer be blindsided.** This is different from over-scripting, where the conversation is excessively controlled; instead we need to do all we can to make sure neither customer is embarrassed or offended. The simplest way to avoid either of these is to ask the prospective customer the top things they are trying to achieve, ask the host customer the things they prefer not to discuss, and make sure both of those things are clear to each party. These are simple rules of engagement: do not over-script but do ensure a high comfort level for your customers.

Simulation Demonstrations

A simulation is a powerful and viable alternative when a live demonstration, for the reasons already discussed, is not possible. In industries where innovation is the norm, this is a common tactic for showing customers how brand-new products and services work. You want to show the customer what they can expect should they buy your product or service that is not yet in use.

In the late 1980s, at HP, we collaborated with Andersen Consulting (AC) in a competition to replace a long-standing IBM system that captured factory workers' time and attendance records on the shop floor. It was a very important project for HP because we were trying to prove to Boeing decision-makers, and other large manufacturing companies, that Open Systems could work in an environment dominated by our competitor.

Top influencers in the IT department had already begun expressing the risks associated with relying on one supplier. They didn't do that on the airplane manufacturing side so why would they do it differently when buying IT products? We emphasized their point and that their years of dependence on one supplier for both hardware and software would soon be over, and that would give them more freedom of choice, and most importantly, improved productivity and added cost savings. Part of the bid process was a "Live Test Demonstration." This was a major hurdle for HP because IBM and other more prominent suppliers were proposing proprietary systems that were already in operation, thus allowing them to demonstrate working deployments inside Boeing.

Demonstrating Innovative Products

Should we win, Boeing would be one of the first major manufacturing companies to use HP-UX, HP's version of the UNIX operating system. Being one of the first meant we had no way to give them a true Live Test Demonstration. We knew that this was a requirement put into the RFP by those who supported our competitors, an example of suppliers influencing the RFP. We had to address this challenge or lose.

As mentioned earlier, we had to create a simulated demonstration. We did a joint proposal with AC (now Accenture) and we decided to set up a mock airplane factory in a large conference room, to simulate a live test demonstration. We treated it just like a factory tour but instead of us conducting a demonstration, we had the Boeing representatives act as factory workers, using our solution as they moved from station to station.

Imagine a large conference room with eight stations in a simulated assembly line. We had plastic model airplanes at each station in varying stages of assembly. The Boeing evaluators checked into our system at the first station by entering their names and employee numbers just as factory workers do, then they would attach a part to the model airplane and mark it completed. They moved through all the stations, attaching another part of the plane and marking it complete. At Stage 4, we simulated a computer failure to demonstrate how our software could automatically, and immediately, switch over to a duplicate system, called a hot spare. Automatic switchover was a requirement for this bid and Boeing was the first to see a demonstration of the product. It worked flawlessly.

(Note: Airplanes and airplane parts are extremely expensive and it takes many people to assemble an airplane. To have the assembly line stop because of a system outage is extremely costly in lost work hours and added inventory carrying costs; fault tolerance or automatic switchover was necessary for Boeing to avoid this costly downtime.)

At each station, we were able to show a key new capability that either addressed a customer concern or touted a feature that our competitor did not offer. At the final station, the Boeing people put a Boeing logo on the model and marked the airplane complete. They logged out and could see a report showing how many person-hours went into building the models, the stage of completion for each unfinished airplane, and how much downtime resulted from the system failure. We added a competition to see which teams assembled their planes the fastest and with the least amount of errors. It made the demonstration a little more fun, which in the long-term helps the customer answer the question, "Would we enjoy working with these people?"

We won that business. Later they told us that they had learned more from the simulated factory than they did walking through a real factory. In actuality, the customers told us that we earned more credibility because we gave them hands-on experience with our hardware and software rather than just walking through a real factory watching other people use it. They also felt it was risky for us to allow them to perform the demonstration themselves. Our willingness to take the risk affirmed our confidence and our CREDABILITY.

The 80/20 Rule of Winning Lifelong Customers

In most cases, 80 percent of what we show customers and clients is the same as what our competitors will show, simply because it is what customers ask for. The creativity and improvisation that makes up the remaining 20 percent is what wins us more business and lifelong customers.

In the previous example that resulted in our winning the business at Boeing, we had no way to show a factory running our solution because it included newly developed technology. This is a common challenge in many industries where constant innovation is at the core of how companies compete. We had to improvise a demonstration that not only showed our new solution, but one that was more memorable to the decision-makers than what they saw from our competitors.

The customers told us they had never had a company present a demonstration that they, rather than the seller, conducted themselves and that made us very memorable. They said it showed that we were very confident that our products would work no matter who was using it. Those kinds of distinctions set us apart from our competition.

Educate

The ability to educate decision-makers and influencers can be the difference between winning and losing with lifelong customers. It's interesting that most customers will not ask you to educate them, beyond the workings of your offering, yet it is usually one of the top purchasing considerations. Why? Because people make business decisions for personal reasons and people benefit, personally, from learning new things and having access to SME salespeople and/or those who have access to SMEs.

In my very first corporate sales job, I sold checks for American Bank Stationery (ABS). Yes, checks—those little pieces of paper that my Millennial-aged kids do not know how to use. At one point in history credit cards were insecure, for reasons other than identify theft, and ATMs were "credit card eaters."

I still believe that job, which I did for almost four years, taught me what real selling is. Those who sell true commodities have to learn what it means to sell yourself, your company, and your product, in that order. My very first sales manager, Jim Kreiter, a great leader and teacher, drilled that into me.

Since checks are just checks, we had to be experts at figuring out why decision-makers at financial institutions would buy from us rather than our biggest competitor, Deluxe Checks, which owned over fifty-five percent of the market. The number-two supplier was Bank Check Supply (BCS), which owned another thirty percent of the market. The rest of us had to split the remaining fifteen percent share, and checks are checks. This is where improvisation counts.

My First Sales Territory

I started as a telesales representative in 1980, in a Portland, Oregon, office covering Alaska, Montana, Wyoming, and Idaho. We did not have LinkedIn or CRM tools (come to think of it, we didn't have computers), but we had printed directories that covered all financial institutions in the country. We had one for each state and they were our lifelines. They listed the institution name, address, phone number, and the top three officers. Even though it was updated every year I called many places that were out of business, asked for people who were no longer there, and in multiple cases, I asked for people who were no longer on earth.

The West Region leadership recognized that our checks alone had no value. Our competition offered significant gifts to customer employees. We had to compete in a different way, which is where I first learned how valuable education is to real decision-makers and influencers.

(Note: Business ethics were much more lax in the early 1980s. It was common for my competitors to give bank executives toasters, televisions, beach holidays, and even Alaskan fishing vacations. We could not compete on that front.)

The goal of all financial institutions was, and still is, to sell more services. They make no profit on savings and checking accounts; instead, they profit when people sign up for loans, credit cards, investment services, etc. The job of New Accounts Representatives was to sell those other services, but in most financial institutions, they did not offer additional services unless customers asked first.

We learned that most New Accounts Representatives thought pitching new services was the equivalent of selling and many felt it was beneath them. Most equated selling with a bad buying experience or with the many negative stereotypes depicted in movies and television.

Armed with this knowledge, our executives had us all certified on Xerox Professional Sales Skills, so we could help New Accounts people be more comfortable when selling. Unfortunately, while attractive to organizational leaders, it was still hard to change the perception by branch personnel that sales and marketing was scary and/or sleazy. Nevertheless, we pursued this education strategy.

Benefitting from My Naivety

What saved me was that I was a naïve twenty-three-year-old who didn't know when to stop. I had called Montana State Credit Union four times, asking for the president each time. Sometimes I got a polite "No." Mostly I got an angry "NO!" On my fifth attempt I was talking to the president's assistant when I heard a man yelling, "Is that the @#$%*@ check guy again? Put that @#$%*@ guy through!"

The president railed about how I was wasting their time and how nobody in Montana was interested in our checks. That I was nothing better than a "used car salesman" (his words) and that I needed to find a real job. He told me I had no value and had no clue about his business. He said, "I need more members who need loans and credit cards. Unless you can make that happen, stop calling. Got it?" Before I could think, I heard my twenty-three-year-old naïve voice saying, "If I can help your new accounts people get more loans and credit card accounts, would you buy our checks?"

He was silent for about five seconds then angrily said, "I should take you up on that just to prove how out of touch you are." I offered a few thoughts on why the average person is scared to sell and how our training addressed that by educating them about sales as a means to help people get what they want.

The president agreed to let me do one training. I had to do it by phone because I had no budget for travel. I came to work on a Saturday morning, as did the New Accounts team in Montana. They were not happy but I found a Dunkin' Donuts nearby their office and that store manager agreed to have one of his people deliver to the credit union if I bought six dozen donuts. That soothed the discontent slightly.

I did an abbreviated ninety-minute training, something we had never done over the phone, and I got agreement from their supervisor to have a follow-up fifteen-minute call the next Friday. Much to my surprise and delight, the following Tuesday I got a call from the credit union president saying his people were actually selling more new services than before we did the training. He asked when I could do another training for his other staff. He also said he would mention our training to his peers in the industry because, "We're all having the same problems."

In less than a year, the Montana territory went from no business to our checks being available at almost half the credit unions in the state. I ended up doing Saturday morning trainings about twice a month. They were not buying the checks; they were buying the sales training. The checks were simply the way they paid us.

I finally met the president of Montana State Credit Union, face-to-face, at a convention in Valdez, Alaska. I was managing our booth and he introduced himself and his New Accounts Supervisor. He said, "You're even younger than I thought." I recognized his voice immediately. He said he wanted to "shake the hand of the pest who helped us improve our new accounts performance even though you were a pest."

His only bad news was that his best new accounts representative left to become a real estate broker. He said that she was the one who was most negative on selling but she found out she was good at it and decided to make it her career. Even so, that president was gracious enough to say to this twenty-three-year-old nobody that he was wrong and that he was happy that I had not given up.

Education is valuable to everyone. When you evolve from seller to educator, you become a relationship that the customer never wants to lose. You start down the path of winning a lifelong customer.

Advocate

There are two elements to manage in regards to advocacy. You want existing customers to consider you reliable enough that they decide to recommend you to their partners, customers, and peers. You want them to advocate for you. This is common knowledge in any business.

The second and most important element of advocacy is for you to advocate for your customers. You, as a trusted advisor, must be genuinely interested in finding the win-win balance between what is best for your customer and what is best for you and your company. Advocating for your customer even before you win the business tells them that your focus is on their success. When you balance this with the needs of your own company, you win lifelong customers without going native—an ultimate win-win.

Advocating for the customer's best interest means that you recommend the best option for their success, which may mean partners, peers, and on occasion, competitors. With the long-term goal of winning lifelong customers there always comes a time when you will not have the best answer to the problem your customer must solve. This does not mean you give up business, but instead, that you bring a solution to the table when your company does not have one to offer.

Advocating for partners and peers who can offer unique help is another way to elevate yourself from seller to advisor. When you advise or consult, introducing other providers shows you as a SME interested in the customer's success. You show that a long-term relationship is important to you even if you do not make a sale today. Advocating for others also shows that you are collaborative and confident enough to bring someone else to the party.

After winning significant business at Boeing, we had the opportunity to win more revenue by including our software development tools. This was in the early days of commercial-off-the-shelf (COTS) software and it was clear that Boeing would be better off buying versus building a solution. The group with whom we worked did not have the expertise to know all of their options and they lacked the expertise to build software. We recommended a software company and did not sell our tools, which earned us lasting credibility leading to years of repeat business.

When you demonstrate, educate, and advocate, you earn unshakable CREDABILITY in the minds of your customers. That

> Demonstrate + Educate + Advocate = Unshakable CREDABILITY.

inevitably leads to more wins and more lifelong customers.

Personal and Professional CREDABILITY

In the customer's eyes, both personal and professional elements of CREDABILITY must be present in order to win business and lifelong customers. Decision-makers and influencers must trust the person selling to them and the company for whom they sell. They must trust the marketing materials, the product guides, the testimonials, etc. That all starts with both the sales staff and everyone across the company doing what is necessary to earn CREDABILITY.

Personal CREDABILITY is really all we have to sell as sales and marketing people; reversing a customer's perception is much harder on a personal level than it is at the company level. Personal CRED**ABILITY** means the customer does not need to go higher in the organization to confirm a commitment because they trust the salesperson.

Doing the Right Thing Is the Only Thing

In the late 1980s, HP came out with new mini-computers running on processors built with Reduced Instruction Set Computing (RISC) technology. Boeing executives chose this new technology for many important programs. It led to the replacement of many existing HP computers even though they still worked well and were viable for many business solutions. When Boeing bought the new RISC-based computers, they put the old systems in storage at the Boeing Stores.

Small program teams could find perfectly adequate equipment in the Boeing Stores and it was free. It did not count as a capital expense, since Boeing already owned it, which meant the free equipment did not have to be justified with ROI or payback analysis. The program teams just had to be the first to claim the equipment and go get it.

When the RISC computers came out we saw many older-technology HP servers end up in the Boeing Stores. At the same time, we had many sales pending to low-profile programs with limited budgets, and as often was the case, we knew more about what was in the Stores than our customers. We had customers trying to justify the purchase of new computers when they could get them free if they just knew about them.

At HP, doing the right thing for the customer was more than a review metric—it was the core of the HP Way. During the days when Bill Hewlett, Dave Packard, John Young, and Lew Platt ran the company, the mantra was that "doing the right thing is the *only* thing." In the HP Way, doing something to cause a customer to lose trust in us was worse than missing our numbers. It wasn't altruistic—it was good business. A happy customer was a repeat purchaser and a willing tester of our innovations. Thus when we knew that our Boeing customers had the option of getting free computers rather than ordering a new one, we told them.

Customers Always Learn the Truth

Once, a competitor's salesperson chided me for being stupid when we gave up a sale by helping a program director configure his computing infrastructure with equipment that was in their stores. We sold a few disk drives for $100,000 rather than a server, disk drives, ports, and terminals for $300,000. However, in the end the customer always discovers the truth, so you have to decide which you would rather explain. Why you didn't let them know how to save money, or why you did? The latter is CREDABILITY.

Our salespeople earned trusted advisor status and from that point, we were no longer vendors. We started getting early information on new projects. We got invites to strategy sessions that determined computer requirements. We went from responding to RFPs to giving Boeing input on what should be in them.

On one major project, the Boeing executives chose me as the only supplier representative on a committee that determined computing requirements for all the commercial computing operations on that program—including which products to buy. I recommended IBM PCs on many occasions, rather than HP's terminals, because at that time they were the best solution. With that earned CREDABILITY, I became a permanent part of the team and nobody challenged me when I recommended HP hardware and software. This was not unique behavior at HP, but instead, was standard practice by many of the great people I got to work with and it all came from the culture created by Hewlett, Packard, Young, and Platt.

Most importantly, in three short years we went from being a small supplier to Boeing Commercial Airplane Group to being a top supplier of commercial servers. In two short years, that territory grew 500 percent and went from one salesperson managing the business to three. HP later became the standard UNIX server supplier to Boeing, which resulted in monthly revenue that was more than our annual revenue when I first joined the team. A team effort founded on the principle that *doing the right thing is the only thing.*

Professional CREDABILITY

Even when a company has a very strong brand, it is irresponsible to assume that the brand alone earns the CREDABILITY necessary for a customer to trust and buy from that company.

In the mid-1990s, Microsoft and Intel were charging forward to win CREDABILITY and market share in the server-computing arena with the Windows Server Operating System and Intel's processors. Microsoft and Intel were trying to disrupt a mature industry that had begun with mainframe computers and had evolved to domination by mini-computers, like the RISC servers I referred to earlier. Mini-computers were replacing mainframes at a fraction of the cost and now Microsoft and Intel were offering servers with microprocessors at even lower cost with higher reliability and increased performance.

Microsoft's challenge was that they had not yet earned the CREDABILITY necessary to compete effectively against stalwarts such as HP, IBM, and DEC. Part of the issue was the newness of the product, but the bigger challenge was the immaturity of the support ecosystem necessary to help companies operate Windows Server environments. Compared to the industry veterans, Microsoft's service offerings were lacking. Later the industry would learn that Windows Server really did not need as much support because of its simplicity and reliability, but the definition of good support was, in those early days, still defined by what the legacy companies had delivered for a generation.

Microsoft was an example of a highly visible, strong brand that had not yet earned the CREDABILITY necessary in this new product area to win significant share. Even the best companies have to do the right things to earn CREDABILITY. Microsoft and their people did eventually become the category experts, but it took a few years and many enhancements to the plans they started with.

CREDABILITY and Social Media

Social media is a powerful tool for delivering value propositions and demonstrating expertise. It is such an omnipresent tool that if you are not productively utilizing it you lack credibility in today's business environment. However, as powerful as social media is, it will not earn you the kind of CREDABILITY that results in winning lifelong customers. To advance from seller to trusted advisor, social media has not yet replaced the credibility of positive human interaction.

When I started my sales career in the early 1980s, salespeople were the primary vehicles through which customers got product information. It was our job to be the SME or to connect customers to SMEs. Today being a SME on our own products is not enough, because customers often know more than we do from what they see on Twitter, LinkedIn, blogs, our websites, competitor's websites, etc. They see how we represent our products and how others depict them. What they cannot assess on social media is whether they can fully trust that you and your company can deliver as depicted online.

More than ever before salespeople must reach the age-old aspirational role of trusted advisor. This is nothing new but it is no longer just an aspiration—it is a requirement. Your ability to provide the kind of value once reserved for consultants is mandatory to earn the CREDABILITY that wins you lifelong customers.

In Summary

When you have customers who are not actively approaching you for advice beyond your products and services, you are not a trusted advisor, and you do not have the CREDABILITY to win lifelong customers. The key to earning CREDABILITY with decision-makers and influencers is to *demonstrate* what you have done or can do, *educate* as a solution SME, and *advocate* for others who can help your customer/client in ways you cannot.

Putting It to Work: Exercises

CREDABILITY – *Showing superior knowledge and success*

Are decision-makers and influencers asking you for business advice beyond what your product/service delivers? Have you transitioned from seller to advisor?   Yes   No

If no:

Have you delivered demonstrations, recommendations, or education that help them see that your value proposition is true and achievable?   Yes   No

If appropriate, have you offered education on your product/service and associated benefits to show your value as an advisor?   Yes   No

Have you advocated for other customers and partners who could help your new customer and have they advocated for you?   Yes   No

For each question you answered "No," describe *why* you think this is happening.

1.

2.

3.

For each reason the answer is no, document your best next
action for changing it to yes.

1.

2.

3.

CHAPTER 4

VIABILITY

OFFERING A SOLUTION THAT FITS THE NEEDS AND READINESS OF BOTH BUYER AND SELLER

Core Indicators That Prove VIABILITY – The NEST Test

Need:

- Goal: Your customer expresses interest/need in the benefit you are selling along with an urgency for solving their known problems that you address.
- Strategy: Create a need, in the mind of the customer, for the benefits afforded by your product or service.

Experience:

- Goal: Customer displays knowledge that shows they have taken on similar challenges before.
- Strategy: Create an opportunity for your customer to comment on your proposal and/or work.

Success:

- Goal: Win against strong competitors.
- Strategy: Customer compares your offering to that of a strong competitor.

Time:

- Goal: Ensure both you and the customer have the time to be successful.
- Strategy: Co-create project plans with customer decision-makers and influencers.

Worse than not winning customers is winning the wrong customers. Most business veterans have experienced situations where a customer is not a good fit, and unfortunately, those are costly. The wrong customer demands more of your resources, they rarely acknowledge a satisfactory result, and they are unwilling and unable to be a reference for your work. Just as it behooves the customer to verify they are buying viable products and services, it is important for you to have a means to ensure that you have a viable customer. We do this by answering a single question:

Is the customer most interested in the expected results rather than the price of your products and services?

When customers challenge your information or ask for clarification that is good news. When you get questions targeting greater understanding or validation of your offering, this indicates you have a customer who sees value in what you are proposing. More curiosity in the evaluation stage typically leads to more loyalty in the long-term because it confirms that they have need for your offering—a key characteristic of a lifelong customer.

Instead, when you have a prospect who focuses mainly on the price of your goods, you have one of three situations:

- The customer thinks you are selling a commoditized offering and the only perceived difference between you and your competition is price. This will never lead to a lifelong customer. (Note: This business could be viable for the short-term if you are strapped for business, but this is most often unsustainable—I recommend against this.)
- The customer is not truly evaluating you but instead they are using you to get your competitor to lower their price. This most often happens when your competition is the incumbent or a mega-brand that the customer has already chosen and they are now trying to strengthen their negotiating position. When you agree to the customer's requested price point and they still have to think about it, this is a key indication that you are being used as a negotiation tool and do not have a real chance at winning the business. A simple question to test for this situation is, "If I agree to your price, what will we be doing tomorrow to get started?" If their answer does not include specific next steps, then you are a negotiation tool or you are not talking to a decision-maker.

- The customer really wants something different from what you offer but they cannot afford it. You are the fallback plan, which means they do not really believe you fully satisfy their needs, and your primary value proposition is price. In most cases, the customer's needs do not change and even though they are paying less, they will evaluate your work based on the product or service they could not afford. This will never result in a lifelong customer unless you can guarantee you will always have the lowest price. A risky place to be.

The true motivations of customers are not always apparent and they often mask what they are really trying to accomplish, whether intentional or not. We need to evaluate four core indicators to determine if the opportunity meets the requirements of **VIABILITY** that, at the very least, lead to profitable business, and at best, lead to lifelong customers.

NEED

You need the customer to articulate the problem they want to solve, why they have it, and how your solution will address it. The customer must proactively, and naturally, express the value they seek and the results they expect from purchasing your product or service. Decision-makers must also have an urgency for getting that result. It is not enough for the customer to answer "Yes" when you ask them if they are looking for certain benefits. You are looking for thoughtful expressions of the value they seek to know that they have real need for your product or service.

If they cannot express their expected value, it does not mean you walk away, but instead that you must develop and deliver a value proposition that allows the customer to seek information from you that confirms their needs. That starts with the exercise we did in Chapter 2 – **VISABILITY**, where we developed a value proposition that creates a suspicion-of-value in the mind of the customer such that they need to learn more. In Chapter 3 – **CREDABILITY**, we amplified that need by showing them how your value proposition can come true when you do the things necessary to demonstrate, educate, and advocate for your offering.

When you understand the customer's problems, you are able to demonstrate products and services in ways that resonate with decision-makers. You are better able to educate in a way that allows customers to see their own needs. You are also able to advocate for other SMEs who can help your customer with their problems while also solidifying the need for your offering.

In the process of confirming the customer has need, it is also important that we ensure their need is not simply a want. This is as common in large and small enterprises as it is in personal buying behaviors—no surprise, since people make business decisions for personal reasons. The difference is the size of the purchase and the number of people affected.

With personal purchases, the cost of deciding on a want versus a need is typically insignificant. For instance, we got a puppy last year and we needed a collar, harness, and leash so he could wear his ID and we could walk him safely. I wanted a Seattle Seahawks 12th Man collar, harness, and leash, which cost a few dollars more and was harder to find, but it addressed my want and the additional expense did not result in an excessive cost other than the rolling eyes of my wife. Business purchases based more on wants than needs not only represent unneeded cash outlay, but also often lead to poor results and negative critique of the decision-maker—your customer. You need to do all you can to help customers avoid such a situation.

Want Versus Need

In the 1990s, it was common for businesses to declare projects as *mission critical*, a military designation made prominent during the early days of space travel. When astronauts were in space, life support and communications were mission critical and could never fail. In response, fault-tolerant and near fault-tolerant computing systems were developed and the era of High Availability (HA) computing was birthed. Systems had to be operational no less than 99.999 percent of the time in order to earn HA designation.

Beyond NASA, the military, and medical facilities, few businesses could justify the need for this kind of technology, but it was the cool thing so everyone wanted it. Everything suddenly became mission critical, especially in high-end manufacturing operations. Unfortunately, HA computing is very expensive because it uses redundancies to accomplish high availability. Essentially, you have two of everything and the extra systems are operational less than 0.001 percent of the time. So if you were going to buy a server for one million dollars (yes, computers cost that much back then), you had to spend almost two million dollars to achieve HA.

We were working with a highly modern facility for a large manufacturer and the plant general manager, Bill, wanted HA computing for his operation. He wanted a "hot spare": a running computer connected to all critical operations that could take over mission-critical operations in fifteen seconds or less, should the main system fail.

Out of 1,500 employees, the plant IT staff along with our engineers identified fifteen users who had mission-critical responsibilities, so we configured a solution for that reality. When Bill learned that the "hot spare" would only cover fifteen users, he was furious. He wanted a solution that would run the whole plant. Bill's team was unsuccessful in helping Bill see want versus need so they asked me to advise him. We had a long conversation at the end of which he said, "This is our most modern facility and I want the best." We showed him that most of his 1,500 employees only used the computer system about ten minutes a day and that the fifteen people we had identified were the only ones who used their systems constantly.

Advise Your Customer on Need Versus Want

We did this in conjunction with his Director of Operations and Director of IT who both agreed with our proposal. We also told Bill that the most common cause for computer downtime was power outage and they had diesel generators that would keep the computers operating indefinitely in case of a total blackout.

We also gave him data that showed the average computer downtime was less than ten minutes when something failed.

We calculated a cost of over one million dollars to achieve full redundancy versus $200K to serve the fifteen users and maintain real-time backup of all data deemed critical. After we had presented our findings Bill said, "OK. I guess we can't justify the cost of full redundancy." He then turned to me and said, "You just gave up $800,000 in sales—you really are a partner."

Some would say I was stupid to give up $800,000 in revenue, but you will never win lifelong customers if you sell things they don't need. One year after that purchase, Bill, who was now a Senior VP, and his Director of Operations, who was now a General Manager of his own plant, shared that selling them just what they needed rather than taking the extra revenue was something they had shared throughout their company. They went on to spend many millions of dollars with HP and rejected many suggestions to consider other suppliers. We had earned a lifelong customer that was worth much more in the long-term than that short-term $800,000.

In corporations, large investments based on wants versus needs can often be troublesome for the decision-maker and their key influencers. When your customer is in trouble and you helped them get there, you lose the opportunity to win and sustain a lifelong customer who will recommend you to other lifelong customers.

EXPERIENCE

You have greater likelihood of success when you have customers with the necessary experience to review your work to help you be better. Experienced customers also understand your advice so they can be better at their business. You have a higher risk of failure when you have customers who are not clear on the successful result they are looking for. Three situations serve as indicators that you have a customer/client who has the right experiences to help you make them successful.

Replacing an incumbent solution (even when it is yours). You are actually better off when competing against a strong incumbent rather than another new player. This may be counterintuitive but when prospective customers have decided to consider new suppliers, their reasons for change are generally clearer than if they are trying to do something they have never done before. They have figured out that they are not addressing a key problem or they are not satisfied with the service and support from the incumbent. In either case, the prospective customer has the experience necessary to evaluate new options and the knowledge to coach a new supplier to success.

Culture of continuous improvement. Decision-makers generally recognize the need for enhancements or modernization because they are not achieving their desired progress in the marketplace. New business wins could be slowing, customer retention could be decreasing, or cost of service and support could be increasing. When these kinds of problems surface, the process of finding solutions gives decision-makers the foundation to understand their own needs, which makes them better prepared to assess new solutions to their problems.

Culture of innovation. There are companies and decision-makers who operate with a culture of constant innovation in both products and ideas. When you see this kind of culture, you tend to find decision-makers who are more comfortable with the unknown. They see discomfort as a reality and an indication of progress rather than risk. The new and unknown represent strengths rather than weaknesses. Customers with this culture are looking for counsel because they operate with the belief that there is always new knowledge to enhance their success. We need not look any further than the evolution of the computing industry to see how a culture of innovation helped to accelerate the use of information technology (IT).

Innovation in Computing

In the 1970s and 1980s, mainframe computing ruled the IT industry. Every major company had a large IT department that managed computing centers with elevated floors, water-cooled mainframes, and air-conditioned rooms that were so cold you could use them to preserve perishable food for days. Imagine the skepticism faced when we introduced mini-computers the size of two-drawer file cabinets that could replace all the computing power they had in rooms the size of a basketball court. Yet, we found people willing to listen because they operated in a culture of innovation.

Again, because the culture of innovation is so prevalent in the IT industry, we had customers with the experience to evaluate our offers and properly counsel us on how best to serve their needs even though they were new to our products and services.

SUCCESS

You should always be nervous when you do not have strong competition. If others are not trying to win the business you are targeting, you have to ask yourself why. It could be that you are first to the party. It could mean that the customer was aware of your company so you simply got the first call. In both cases, you will likely have competition and that's a good thing.

Most often, you know the major competitors in the industry and the geography you cover. You have done your homework to know their value propositions and their reasons for presenting themselves as the best choice. Today, since most companies host websites or blogs and have LinkedIn profiles, it is very simple to deduce the competitors' selling points. Knowing these selling points allows you to listen for them in the questions the customers ask.

The Commercial Server Industry

In the commercial server industry, the market leaders were International Business Machines (IBM) and Digital Equipment Corporation (DEC). IBM's messaging focused on safety and simplicity. The old slogan was, "Nobody ever gets fired for choosing IBM." As the market leader, they offered the most comfort to decision-makers who were more interested in smooth sailing than innovative changes. IBM was the low-risk option and competitors' salespeople could hear it in the questions customers asked:

- Will you guarantee uninterrupted transition?
- Can you show us where others have been successful by choosing you?
- Will our people be able to use your system without any training?
- How do we get emergency support? Are you available 24/7?
- How many times have you done this? Are you experienced or experimenting?
- Are you a safe bet for whoever makes the decision?

These kinds of questions were a good indication that IBM was the chief competitor and it guided us on how to build successful value propositions and presentations directed at their offerings.

If DEC was the chief competition, the questions were more like:

- Can you guarantee 99.9 percent uptime?
- Are your development tools easy to use?
- Will college graduates know how to use your development tools? (DEC was very prominent on college campuses, so in the 1980s most college graduates had worked on DEC systems.)
- Will we be able to reduce our computing costs by 10-20 percent?
- Why does your competition offer more but charge less?

When we got these questions, we knew our competition was DEC. If we got any questions regarding fault tolerance or redundant systems, we knew our competition was either Tandem or Sequent. On the rare occasion where we could not detect the presence of strong competition, we had to find out why.

The most common reasons for the endless questions:

- The customer is a perpetual analyzer consuming much time but never making a buying decision.
- The customer uses buying signs simply as a means to test what is new but rarely makes changes.
- The people you work with are not decision-makers or influencers as they had introduced themselves.

In all cases, we are better off having strong, known competition rather than pursuing business that nobody else wants.

TIME

A very common cause of project failure comes when the seller—and/or the customer—does not allow enough time for a successful outcome. At today's speed of business, everyone wants to complete projects and programs faster. Time-to-market is an advantage everyone is looking for and it's tempting to think we can just assign more resources to speed up the process, especially when the competition commits to a shorter time-to-market.

The main problem with overcommitting on time-to-market is that the customer does not find out until it is too late. They choose your offering and by the time they learn the project is going to be late, they have already invested in you and they cannot recover the time and resource.

Consequences of Not Having the Time to Be Successful

The City of Seattle is a good example of the foibles of over-committing and under-delivering. Seattle has undertaken a mammoth tunnel project to replace an elevated road on the Puget Sound waterfront. The Alaskan Way Viaduct is a dilap-idated eyesore to those with condominiums or offices on the Seattle waterfront. The project will replace the elevated road with a tunnel that allows people to make the same trek, but underground.

The tunnel was supposed to open by 2015,[3] but through a series of miscalculations, unexpected challenges, and equipment failures, the project is already years behind schedule. Now everyone that is associated with the project is getting bad press, including the contractors and city leaders who awarded the contract. In talking with those who have knowledge of the challenge, most foresaw that the timelines were unrealistic and that no amount of investment could accelerate the timeline. Unfortunately, the City of Seattle demanded a 2015 completion.

In the end, who gets most of the blame for the delay? The people and companies who sold the solution, of course. Sure, the news media will talk about the leaders who were too aggressive in their timelines, but it is always a losing proposition for the seller to blame the buyer for a failure. As such, missed deadlines become the fault of suppliers, which lessens or eliminates the possibility of winning again. You also significantly diminish opportunities with any observers who may have otherwise been solid prospective customers.

You need to ensure that you have the time to complete your commitments. The best way is to walk through a project plan with the customer so they see for themselves exactly what they are asking you to do. By doing this you present yourself as an advisor, and through the review you get a better understanding of what the competition is proposing. Both allow you to compete better.

In Summary

NEST is a tool you can use to remember these key checkpoints to determine if you have a viable customer and if you are viable for them:

- If the customer or client cannot articulate their **NEED** for your offering, then you have more convincing to do.

- If they do not have the **EXPERIENCE** necessary to evaluate, coach, and correct, you might be setting yourself and your customer on a path to failure.
- When a prospective customer does not represent **SUCCESS** such that competitors also want their business, you need to re-evaluate whether this is good business for you.
- If **TIME** to market is unrealistic, you are better off to forewarn the customer rather than allowing them to have mistaken expectations. Saying nothing is equal to overcommitting.

Final Caveat

You will find yourself in situations where you have large opportunities that you are not able to pass up. You must balance your need and desire for today's business with the long-term success of winning lifelong customers. If walking away from business leaves you out of the running forever, it might be better to compete, even if the business does not meet all the characteristics of **VIABILITY**. Making those judgment calls is always part of the sales challenge. However, in most enterprise selling situations we do a service to our customers—and ourselves—by ensuring we are a viable fit for each other.

Putting It to Work: Exercises

VIABILITY – Offering a solution that fits both your customer's needs and your collective readiness to execute.

Are discussions with decision-makers mostly about results rather than price?   Yes   No

If no:

Have decision-makers and influencers identified their needs that your product/service addresses?   Yes   No

Do they have enough experience and expertise to assess your performance?   Yes   No

Are decision-makers and influencers considering other options? Does this customer have enough success history that competitors are also pursuing them?   Yes   No

Do you both have the time and budget necessary for your product/service to show results?   Yes   No

For each no, document why you think this is happening.

1.

2.

3.

4.

For each reason why the answer is no, document your best next action for changing it to yes.

1.

2.

3.

4.

CHAPTER 5

CAPABILITY

DELIVERING WHAT THE CUSTOMER BUYS THAT IS NOT ON THE INVOICE

People make business decisions for personal reasons. You must understand the personal motivations of decision-makers and influencers, in order to deliver the CAPABILITY

> *People make business decisions for personal reasons.*

they look for in choosing from whom to buy.

Can you articulate the personal wins that decision-makers and influencers are looking for? If the answer is no, you have not yet learned all that is necessary to earn CAPABILITY with your customer or client.

The only way to deliver the right CAPABILITY is to know and address the personal motivations of the people in charge—the decision-makers and influencers. Marketing materials, including your presentations and demonstrations, most often focus on corporate and organizational motivations—the things you see in ROI calculations and balance sheets. This is natural because mass marketing addresses general need. Social media sometimes has better focus when combined with big data analytics, but marketing, by necessity, aims at the large general audience. It is up to salespeople to uncover and address personal motivations for buying.

Personal Motivations for Buying That Earn CAPABILITY Are:

Safety, Simplicity, Rewards, Recognition, and Revolution

Safety motivates people who ...

- ... cannot afford a mistake.
- ... must avoid a negative outcome for themselves and/or their teams.
- ... are naturally risk averse.

Simplicity motivates people who ...

- ... want to reduce workload and stress for both themselves and their teams.
- ... want to offload repetitive but necessary tasks.
- ... want to avoid having to learn something that will not be critical in the future.

Reward motivates people who ...

- ... view promotions and an upward career trajectory as rewards for a job well done.
- ... view compensation as a way to measure their own success.
- ... view awards as a way to recognize their own – and their team members' – accomplishments.

Recognition motivates people who ...

- ... value being subject matter experts (SME).
- ... value being great teammates.
- ... enjoy helping others via advice, mentorship, etc.

Revolution motivates people who ...

- ... seek out change.
- ... desire to be change agents.
- ... seek to create a legacy for themselves and/or their team.

Companies Don't Make Decisions — People Do

You necessarily learn the details on how to communicate the capabilities and benefits of your products and/or services. You show how your products increase revenue and profits while decreasing time-to-market and costs. Your data shows how customers will be more satisfied once the company adopts your product. Your presentations and demonstrations typically focus on things measured within the general metrics included in income statements, balance sheets, ROI analyses, and customer surveys.

All this is good—however, addressing the company needs for increased productivity, better efficiencies, and increased revenue are only part of the decision-maker's criteria for choosing from whom they buy. In reality, no matter how long the list of business requirements, *companies do not make decisions, people do*. In order for you to get decisions made in your favor, and more importantly to earn lifelong customers, you must learn and address the personal motivations of decision-makers and key influencers.

It is easy to learn the needs of the business—things we discover on spreadsheets and requests for proposals. However, this is the least impactful piece of the sales puzzle when trying to win business in ultra-competitive environments because our competitors are focusing on the same things. In essence, if we stick just to business needs we are selling what everyone else is selling. This is increasingly so in today's world of lightning-fast product and service knowledge transfer.

The more impactful and complex part of the puzzle is the personal motivation driving the decision-makers and those close advisors with whom they surround themselves. The personal motivations for buying are not part of RFPs or requirements documents. Often the people influencing the decision even misrepresent their personal motivations in the form of business and organizational needs. Instead, you must discover personal motivations by developing relationships with decision-makers and the people around them—the most valuable and fun part of selling, in my opinion.

Let us identify the five primary personal motivations for buying, and then study examples where people have unintentionally misrepresented their motivations.

Safety

Many decision-makers in this category seek to obtain more job security for themselves and their team. These kinds of decision-makers are often in companies that are downsizing or in organizations that have underperformed in the recent past. More broadly, some companies have risk-averse cultures that are very steadfast in the ways they do business causing them to make change in very small increments. In these environments, avoiding mistakes is more valuable than learning from mistakes.

These corporate cultures tend to promote leaders who are more risk-averse and who tend to take the safe route on decisions. Even so, most leaders will not identify themselves as risk-averse whether they are or not. This is especially true in Western cultures where many want to maintain an image of courage and fearlessness, whether that is their true motivating personality or not. Meryl Streep's character in the movie *The Devil Wears Prada*[4] or Mark Harmon's character in the television show *NCIS*[5] are the stereotypical images that leaders in Western cultures often want to emulate.

They want to represent an image of someone who is courageous, hard-charging, risk-taking—someone who is comfortable with marching aggressively into the unknown. "No risk, no reward," and "No pain, no gain," are common mantras you will hear throughout these corporate populations, whether or not they represent actual behavior. How do you determine when a decision-maker is a seeker of safety, and how do you satisfy their needs?

The good news about safety-focused decision-makers is that most people surrounding them will know that they lean towards safe, low-risk decisions. The people who the decision-maker depends on most know that they have to help the leader make safe decisions in order to remain in their advisory circle.

When you see interactions in groups led by a safety-motivated leader, you will hear many "what-if" questions in meetings. You will oftentimes see meetings end with more questions than answers because those who buy safety want the answer to all questions, thus averting all risk before making a decision. You will also get more requests for guarantees in the areas of product functionality, support services, and results.

Risk-Averse Leaders Still Get Things Done

I had a great business manager who had a lot of decision-making authority within my group. She came from both a family and a business culture that emphasized the virtue of not making mistakes. She was an incredibly smart and effective leader but she had a risk-averse quirk that was especially prevalent when she was spending the company's money. I valued this trait a lot, and I knew that with her watching my budget I would never overspend.

However, her style presented challenges to teammates, partners, and suppliers. No matter how much experience they brought to the table and no matter how many times they had delivered for us before, she wanted to know every detail to avoid any chance that we would overspend the allotted budget for a project. Even more important to her was that anything she chose to invest in had to work—she was highly averse to failure. In her mind, there was no room for mistakes if she was the decision-maker, and on the few occasions where she was human and did falter, I could see the self-imposed pain on her face.

The people, both internally and externally, who were successful in getting her approval on new investments were those who gave her the most complete information and those who were the most responsive to her complicated and sometimes seemingly paranoid "what-if" questions. The people who most often won with her were those who showed patience and the attention to detail that she expected of herself.

The way you sell to safety-focused decision-makers is to be extra attentive and responsive to their questions. Quick, complete answers tell a risk-averse leader that you have solved this problem before and that there is no reason to worry. Answer a question without sufficient supporting information or take too long to respond, and these kinds of decision-makers see risk even if there is none. The worst thing to do with these kinds of decision-makers is to surprise them, so you need to work closely with advisors who can help you anticipate areas of concern.

This kind of decision-maker is also more comfortable when there are people in the boat with them. With my business manager, it was often enough just to emphasize that I would be standing right there with her no matter what the result. She just needed reassurance that her boss had her back. You will find many very successful and productive decision-makers and influencers just like her.

(Warning: Salespeople occasionally see safety-motivated decision-makers and decide they are not real decision-makers. This stems from the Western business culture of high-risk/high-reward. Be careful in making this assessment because many leaders empower safety-focused decision-makers because careless mistakes are not tolerable at a given point in time. Never sell these people short because they are generally in place for good reason.)

Simplicity

Most leaders are willing to make investments if the result is simplification of their operations. Simplification can lead to cost reductions and margin enhancements—traditional business goals. The difference between wanting simpler operations and having it be a primary motivator gets to a personal level. It is about a person's desire to reduce or remove confusion and increase predictability for themselves and the people around them.

Unlike safety, this trait is not easy to identify because often the decision-maker does not know that there are simpler ways to do things. This is where your CREDABILITY as a business advisor comes in as part of the selling process. When you see an organization that is constantly rushing, people who regularly cancel meetings, and people who work longer than normal hours, you are typically looking at an organization that could somewhere benefit from simplicity.

Selling to a Simplicity-Focused Leader

I had a customer at a large company in Seattle who not only had an incredible career as one of the top executives in the company, but she also made quite a contribution to her community. Her parents were famous in the Seattle area, and one of the priorities that they instilled in their kids was the importance of giving back to the community. She coached both her daughters' soccer teams but was also very involved in a local chapter of the American Heart Association (AHA).

As successful as she was, she always wanted to do more for her community. It caused her deep pain to be late to one of her girls' soccer games or to have to miss a meeting for the AHA. Even though she did more than most of us, she only wanted to do more. That drive and her smarts are what made her successful at Boeing and everything else she did.

I got to know her through AHA fundraising, and ironically, I never sold her anything—but through that relationship, I did find business for other people at HP and some of the consultants we partnered with. I just never had the right thing to sell her to simplify her business life, but after a few fundraising events with the AHA she told me that having me on her volunteer team "makes my life a lot easier."

While I never sold anything to her department, she often recommended me to other executives and her endorsement turned into much business for HP and me. She often told me how the consultants who I had introduced to her had shaved time off her workday. They helped her refine some of her team's processes and implemented software tools that minimized her "busy work," therefore making her more available for her employees, family, and community service projects.

The measurement of success may be as simple as seeing people leave work earlier. A reduction in emergency actions is another way I have seen this measured, and like with safety, people who want simplicity also hate surprises. This is probably the most obvious thing that their team members and advisors observe because they can see the decision-maker's irritation when they see longer workdays brought on by surprise requirements, like learning at 6:00 p.m. on Monday that an assignment originally due on Friday is now due on Tuesday. (Yes, that happened to me—multiple times.) The difference between the reaction by safety-focused leaders and simplicity-focused leaders is that the former fear for their jobs while the latter show annoyance at the loss of time that keeps them from contributing in other ways.

Rewards

Decision-makers in this category are typically the easiest to spot. These people wear their careers on their sleeves and everyone around them knows it. These are the people who many will describe as highly political and who some will even call narcissistic because they seem to always be thinking about their own career instead of looking for how they can help others grow. While this may seem negative, it is not. It's just how some people measure their contribution, both in their personal and business lives.

The reality is that these "career missiles" do think a lot about how they help the people around them, because decision-makers in this category have a hard time thinking that anyone would work hard for any reason other than a promotion or some kind of visible reward. We can see this reward motivation demonstrated by how the people in the organization talk and the way they measure success. They will talk about the time between promotions or how long before they have more responsibility.

What Is It Like to Work with Career Missiles?

I have worked for many great managers throughout my years and the ones who were motivated by their own career growth would build career momentum into my reviews. They would ask me how long I expected to be at my current level and help me identify things I needed to accomplish or improve in order to earn promotions. Even though promotions were never my primary motivation, these leaders found ways to get me promoted faster because it was a way they measured their own success. This is another environmental characteristic to look for because the people who work around these kinds of leaders tend to get promotions and awards more often.

I also had a peer who was very career-minded. When we began working together, he had been with the company longer than I had and was taking on his first assignment outside of a product management role. He managed our marketing department, and to this day, is one of the most creative people I have ever worked with. He, like many corporate leaders, wore his career on his sleeve and was very intent on doing big things that attracted a lot of attention.

In marketing, we tended to hire many consultants during product launches because the workload soars, only to decline greatly after the launch. My peer hired a consulting firm that specialized in graphics and videos for training salespeople and channel partners. He was very excited about the opportunities offered by this company and presented it to the rest of the leadership team. The presentation got good response, in particular from the VP who ran our division, and that was all it took for my peer to be off and running with this new way of training our sales force and our channel.

His team produced thousands of DVDs with all the new content while also making it available online. It was great marketing material but because it was so voluminous, it was hard for our sales and marketing people to use. While it was beautiful work, nobody was using it. That great work never delivered value because it was impractical. All of us worked to find ways for this marketing material to be more useful to our field and channel, but when it was clear that it was going to fail, that peer no longer associated himself with the project, leaving sales management and the consultant to shoulder the responsibility.

These kinds of leaders are not bad people, but this behavior is more common than you might believe. They just have different personal motivations than others. The main message here is that when we sell to decision-makers who are motivated by rewards, it is good to have other mentor-like relationships in the customer's company so you have a shoulder to lean on if you sense the original decision-maker is losing interest.

To ensure you remain on a successful path, even in the face of a disappearing decision-maker, you benefit from developing associated relationships with key influencers who are motivated by recognition. The wins of recognition seekers are very different from those of reward seekers, but they are often complementary because they help each other. Because of this, you can help each simultaneously, which enhances your probability of success and reduces the risk of ending up without a sponsor or advocate.

Recognition

Many initially see reward and recognition as the same but they are very different. People who thrive on recognition, enough that it drives their decision-making, are those who are looking to be the expert and/or the ultimate team player. The one who others come to for help. The person that people often choose as a mentor.

These people are almost the opposite of reward seekers in that they do not see promotions or awards as something to strive for, but instead see them as confirmation that they are making positive contributions to their team and others around them. Recognition-seekers are also easy to identify because their names surface when you ask people whom they seek for help. When you ask to know more about a business, the names of these people will come up as SMEs with whom you need to talk.

People Who Are Recognition Decision-Makers Often Don't Know It

A good friend of mine managed a global team of over 300 people. He was known as customer-focused, a creative problem solver, and someone who was an expert on our business. He was early to step up when a problem needed solving. He also was often the last person out of the building at night because he would spend his days in business meetings and mentoring sessions. He spent his nights catching up on things he could not finish during the day.

If you asked him to describe his personal motivations for making decisions, including purchasing decisions, he would tell you that he is constantly trying to find ways to simplify the challenges for his people. My friend clearly felt his personal motivations were all about making life simpler for him and his teams—simplicity. However, as is often the case, when you asked people who knew him well, it was clear that being the expert and a great team player were core values for this decision-maker. His door was always open, and people in and out of his organization relied on him for coaching.

These people tend to become experts in their area of business in order to be the ultimate team players that help others succeed. Not only can they conduct the business well, but they can also explain why they and their team are successful and why they are not. These people rise in the organization, but perhaps not as fast as reward seekers, and they do it more quietly. They are more apt to let news of their promotions trickle out rather than making a big announcement because, again, this is not a primary motivation. This trait will help you identify recognition seekers.

(Note: Reward seekers and recognition seekers make good partners and you will often find them to be good friends within an organization. The reward seeker helps recognition seekers get promotions and awards. The recognition seeker helps the reward seeker stay on track to their promotions when problems start to mount. This is a good win-win team to find among your customers.)

Revolution

Have you ever met someone who, from day one, wants to change everything? I think we have all met someone like this, and they serve an important purpose. These are people good at solving problems that require taking huge risks.

While leaders who strive for safety and simplicity want small incremental changes, these leaders want big revolutionary change that often seems unrealistic. Part of this is because they hate the status quo. Another reason is that they want to make their marks. They want to leave a legacy of accomplishment and they cannot be satiated unless they reconstruct the mission of the organization and the way it operates. Again, this is simply the way these people learned to define "contribution." It is also valuable, particularly in young companies that have yet to reach their potential.

Hot Rod

I had the opportunity to work for a great person whom I will call Rod. He had managed multiple country teams before moving to headquarters, where he took over the leadership of the OEM group, which was then the largest business unit at Microsoft. The growth rate of the OEM Division was slowing for the first time since the company's founding. Rod was the CEO's choice to get the business back to historical growth rates.

Rod spent the first three months meeting with customers and learning about the business from all of us. His leadership team consisted of seventeen people, over half of whom had spent more than ten years in the business. Many of us thought we knew everything about our business; however, after circling the globe multiple times Rod informed us that, "You guys have totally underestimated how fast PC usage is growing in emerging markets. We are missing a huge opportunity. The old ways of doing business don't apply anymore."

Within six months after that meeting, he had either removed or demoted nine of the seventeen members on his leadership team. He got approval to make significant investments in what we called emerging markets. Those of us who were fortunate enough to stay understood that what made us successful in the past would no longer be satisfactory to this new leader or to Microsoft. Looking at his history, we could have predicted that this would happen: that he would do his research and then develop a new strategy based on what he learned through customer and employee engagement.

It's common to find these kinds of leaders in turnaround roles. When you look at their history, you will see where they took over organizations with poor results. You will also see a history of organizational changes in structure and people. People driven by revolutionary change often feel they cannot do it with the people who were there before. They want new blood, even when their existing staff is full of top performers.

The good news for salespeople is that these are typically the risk takers who will readily invest to make things better—or at least *seem* better. You need to watch out for the second scenario because it rarely works out when you invest in projects that do not really accomplish anything. That usually keeps us from getting repeat business after the current leader is off to his or her next revolution.

When dealing with this category of decision-maker, we sometimes have to save them from their own ambition by being trusted advisors and consultants who are willing—and able—to help them understand the barriers that may slow their revolution.

In Summary

Remembering two realities helps us be more capable for our customers and clients: First, companies do not make decisions—people do. Second, people make business decisions for personal reasons and what they buy is not on the invoice. To be consistent winners we need to be good at spotting the personal motivations of decision-makers so we can show our **CAPABILITY** to deliver their personal win.

Leaders rise to their positions because they make good decisions based on their unique motivations and instincts that are often not on income statements and balance sheets. These are also the decision-makers who, when satisfied, make for lifelong customers because they choose to do business with people who know how to help them satisfy their personal motivations.

Putting It to Work: Exercises

CAPABILITY – Delivering what the customer buys, before and after making the sale.

Do you know the personal motivations for buying of decision-makers and influencers? Yes   No

If no, assess from the following what you believe is motivating each decision-maker and influencer:

- Safety – These people ask for guarantees. They ask "what if this goes wrong" questions. They are risk-averse. They fear failure either because it is their nature or because their position is threatened. Do you have customers motivated by safety?
Yes   No   (If yes, list them here.)

- Simplicity – These people want to see reduced workload for themselves and their team. They are clear on expected results but expect you to deliver results without much supervision. If they have to be deeply involved with every detail, they will be unhappy because you have not made their life simpler. Do you have customers motivated by simplicity?
Yes   No   (If yes, list them here.)

- Reward – These people expect something good to happen for them when your products/services deliver successful results—promotions, bonuses, awards, etc. These people want to be involved in the day-to-day, want regular formal updates, and are milestone-driven. They get testy when they feel out of the loop or unclear about progress. Do you have customers motivated by reward?
Yes   No   (If yes, list them here.)

- Recognition – These people want to be the persons who get things done. They want to be great teammates. They enjoy being the one who others come to for help or coaching. Others see these people as subject matter experts (SMEs). Do you have customers motivated by recognition?
Yes   No   (If yes, list them here.)

- Revolution – These people are in place to make change and they like it. You will hear these people talk about innovation or reinventing. These people are bored by incremental improvements and do not consider them true change. Others describe these people as innovative and as change agents. Do you have customers motivated by revolution?
Yes   No   (If yes, list them here.)

List all customers for which you answered yes along with their motivation and why you classified your customer(s) as such:

For each reason why, document your best next action for addressing the customer's personal motivations for buying:

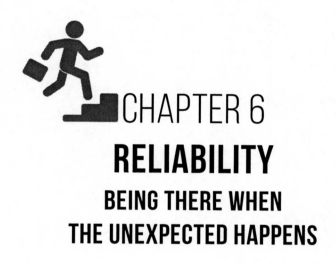

CHAPTER 6
RELIABILITY
BEING THERE WHEN
THE UNEXPECTED HAPPENS

In all businesses and in all industries, no matter how good our intentions or how complete our proposals, unexpected problems will arise—and the unexpected comes in many forms. Our product may not perform as expected. The customer may not have the experience necessary to complete a project. The customer's company has a leadership change resulting in new priorities. The list is truly endless, but our response is the same no matter what: we have to take accountability for whatever happens to ensure we demonstrate a culture of RELIABILITY and no surprises.

What Does It Mean to Have a "Culture of No Surprises?"

You are unreasonably accountable:

- You do not confuse accountability with responsibility.
- You are accountable for whatever happens next, whether we caused it or not.
- You work on the same side of the table with the customer.

You are always predictable:

- Ensure that your customer never has to wonder if you will perform as promised.
- Be there when they expect you to be there.
- Be available at unreasonable times.

You anticipate challenges:

- Know your customer better than they know themselves – anticipate their needs.
- Know your customer's other suppliers; be a good collaborator.
- Know the trends of your customer's industry to stay ahead of important events.

You communicate good news and bad news equally:

- Good news is easy/bad news is hard – choose the hard path.
- Be first to communicate bad news that pertains to you.
- Your competitors win when they communicate your mistakes. Do not let them win.

Being dressed down can dress you up:

- Customers are people too. Let them vent – listen without being defensive.
- An angry customer is often an open and honest customer – a great opportunity to learn.
- An angry customer more openly displays their personal motivation for buying.

Unreasonably Accountable

It is critical that you understand the practice of RELIABILITY on your way to winning lifelong customers. This is important as it regards business generally, and sales specifically. It is doubly crucial that you guard against the misconceptions that exist around this very important ability.

First, we need to look at how people respond to the notion of being accountable—no matter what. What I often observe, when addressing this **ABILITY**, is that people reject it. What I have learned after many years of managing people is that they hear *accountable* but they think *responsible*. They respond negatively because they are defending themselves from blame for an undesired result. Let us define the two words in the context of business.

- *Responsible* – Being responsible for a business result has two meanings. The present tense is that we own the performance of an assignment, project, or team. The past tense is that we were the cause for something that happened.
- *Accountable* – Being accountable for something in a business sense means that we own whatever happens next. We are in charge of the best next action. Whether we caused the problem or not, we step up to own the solution.

Customers/clients appreciate responsible salespeople—they buy from those who are accountable. The former shows up on time, follows through on commitments, and answers questions to their best ability. The latter does all those things but takes ownership of the buyer's positive outcome and just gets things done. You want to be the latter.

Unreasonably Accountable In Action

Rob is one of the most customer-centric people I have had the privilege to work with. His nature, in life and in business, is to be unreasonably accountable.

Early in his career, Rob worked for a company that offered component manufacturing and supply chain services to a myriad of technology companies. One of his customers was a prominent computer manufacturer and he was competing for their business against a deeply entrenched incumbent service provider. In this case, Rob had convinced the decision-maker to trial his company's storage devices and had an initial order shipped from Raleigh, North Carolina, to the customer's location in Norfolk, Virginia. Ironically, because the incumbent was managing the project, Rob found himself delivering product to his competitor.

As luck would have it, the shipment of storage devices incurred damage in transit. Rob, of course, immediately got on the phone with the project manager (his competitor) in the hopes of understanding what happened so he could determine his best next action for resolving the problem. The competitor was unclear about what had happened and was generally unhelpful. Rob hung up the phone with no more clarity about the situation than before he made the call.

Rob had a manager who instilled in him a lifelong discipline that said, "If you have a problem, get to the problem." After brief consideration, Rob decided to get to the problem. He was able to get co-workers to complete tasks he had been assigned and he got in his car to drive the 184 miles to Norfolk, so he could learn firsthand what had happened to those storage devices. He not only was able to resolve the issue but he demonstrated the act of being unreasonably accountable to the decision-makers. That best next action led to Rob earning more business, and winning over decision-makers who became lifelong customers.

Being unreasonably accountable is about taking the best next action when your customer needs help. When your customer has a problem, whether you caused it or not, if you are capable of helping, do it. You step up because you want to help your lifelong customers—not because you want accolades but because you are unreasonably accountable.

Being Predictable

In business, being predictable is often more important than being good. Take Wall Street for example, where performance that exceeds leadership's predictions can be bad news because investors prefer managers who can accurately forecast results for their business. As with Wall Street investors, decision-makers and influencers hate surprises—even good ones. What matters more is that you know enough about your offer and their business to forecast results accurately. More importantly, you walk your talk. You are predictable.

Some think that being predictable is boring. In dating, predictability may be boring in a bad way, but when it comes to business, decision-makers prefer boring. High-level decision-makers have to deal with daily surprises caused by changes in customer demands and industry competition. Unexpected occurrences are a necessary reality that all leaders have to deal with. You, as a lifelong problem-solver and supplier, should never be a constant source of surprises.

Predictable Integrity

In 2000, I became the director managing Microsoft's OEM alliance with Dell Corporation. I left my post as Group Manager of the HP relationship, and as was common practice, we informed Dell's executives of my background prior to my move. (It was standard practice for Microsoft to give major customers a voice in who would manage their relationship. It was important that they know I worked with their chief competitor, in my previous role, and that they had the option to reject me.)

On my first trip to Dell's headquarters, I met with Tom, their executive responsible for the overall Microsoft relationship. I entered his office, and he walked around his desk to shake hands and exchange niceties. He then asked, "What do you think about PwC?" PwC stands for PricewaterhouseCoopers, and at the time, the business press had leaked a rumor that HP planned to acquire them.

At Microsoft, as with most technology companies, it is a firing offense to share confidential information—especially about a customer. It is obviously wrong to share information a customer has shared in confidence. When he asked me the question I simply said, "It'll be interesting to see if the press is right." The executive smiled and we moved on to talk about what he considered the top priorities of Dell's leadership team. I listened, shared Microsoft's priorities, and we ended the meeting.

A few months later, I met with one of Dell's sales VPs to discuss a confidential topic. He said that we could talk, "because you got a clean bill of health from Tom." I asked what that meant. He said that I had declined to share what I knew about HP's acquisition of PricewaterhouseCoopers even though a friend of Tom's, at HP, had told him I had been part of the pre-acquisition discussions, because PwC would be providing consulting services for Microsoft products.

In short, I was predictable in the area of confidentiality. There were a few other instances where the team was able to confirm that we could maintain confidentiality. Our whole team earned the monikers of "predictable and trustworthy" by Dell executives.

Anticipate and Act On Challenges

This is a close cousin to being predictable; the difference is that you have now moved beyond what you can control. Anticipating challenges demands that we constantly study our customers and the industries in which they belong. This is not easy, but it is simpler now because of the wealth of information we can find on the Internet.

For those selling to Fortune 100 companies or well-known innovative small businesses, you have a small advantage because your customer will typically be in the news. However, if you only read the news that is on the Internet, you will be behind your competitors who are also trying to win business with your future lifelong customers.

For this reason, continual networking inside the customer's company is critical. As salespeople, we often have a broader view of what is happening in our customer's own company than they do, simply because political barriers do not block us. In large companies, many people have an easier time sharing key information with a trusted outside advisor than they do with their own peers. It is an unfortunate reality of corporate politics, but it is also a key opportunity for you as a trusted advisor.

The HP Way

As mentioned, in the early 1980s, I was fortunate to sell for one of the most customer-focused companies at the time: HP. I was on a global account team and our customer was Boeing. The HP Way taught us to treat *everyone* like a customer. We were to help teammates, when possible, and to anticipate their needs, just as we would in our relationships with real customers.

Back then, there were many changes occurring in the computer industry. Not the least of which was the introduction of PCs and the introduction of the UNIX operating system. These new technologies allowed customers to build custom applications that would run across multiple computing platforms, so for the first time customers could buy or build software that would work on all computers. Before this, customers had to use the hardware of the company that built the software applications.

HP leadership anticipated that this change would encounter skepticism so they taught us how to talk about the benefits of UNIX and PCs over proprietary systems and dumb terminals. For about a year our team was constantly identifying decision-makers who were skeptical and who wanted an explanation from someone other than their own internal sources. To be clear, it was not due to a lack of trust in their own people, but a desire to hear different pros and cons so they could make good decisions regarding this significant technology innovation.

The ability for HP, then under the leadership of the legendary Lew Platt, to anticipate the need for education and to deliver it well earned us a consultative position that we did not have before. When you know your customers and the industry well enough to anticipate and act on challenges that effectively merge your knowledge with their needs, you are on the path to earning lifelong customers.

Aggressively Communicate Bad News

Reliable sellers are always the first to notify the customer when something unexpected happens, or even more important, when something disruptive is going to happen. Conversely, unreliable sellers let the customer find out on their own. High-level decision-makers want to work with people and companies that are confident enough to own up to their mistakes and/or shortcomings.

One of the most common causes of tension between a supplier and a lifelong customer is when the customer thinks you are not being honest with them. An obvious statement, but there are many things that can cause a loss in trust, not the least of which is a perceived unwillingness to directly and clearly deliver bad news. This is a critical part of creating a culture and expectation of no surprises. Being willing to gracefully, but completely, communicate bad news is a big component of earning lifelong customers.

However, here you must walk the fine line of "I'm sorry." If you say you are sorry too much, the customer will perceive that you are always making mistakes. You should never think of this as something that gains favor. The purpose for aggressively communicating bad news is to work with the customer to get ahead of whatever problems may be coming, not to simply show you feel badly about your mistakes. Proactively communicating about problems is more about management discipline than it is about continually showing how much you regret being incorrect.

On-the-Job Learning: Communicating Bad News

I actually learned this principle at a very early age working in construction, for my uncle, at a summer job during college. He was building a hotel in Portland, Oregon, and he let me and a friend, Jon, do odd jobs on the construction site.

The hotel was on schedule to open in late summer but the building failed a fire code inspection because of a gap between walls in the laundry chute that stretched from the basement to the top of the building. The gap was only an inch wide but you could feel air coming through the crack. The fire inspectors said it was a hazard.

The construction crew had many ideas to fill the gap including rebuilding what was effectively a cement chimney that went through the center of the building. I knew nothing about construction but I was a nineteen-year-old invincible, so I suggested I just climb up the shaft and plug the gap with fireproof material. I knew how to shimmy up walls from rock-climbing, and because there was an opening on each floor, I could rope up with my friend as a belaying partner. It would be safe. The construction crew dismissed it, but it was the quickest solution so my uncle told us to give it a shot.

We made one attempt with a fire retardant material, but when I got to the top of the building, I could still feel air coming through. We reported the result to the site supervisor telling him I did not think it would work. I also gave him an alternative of putting cement in the gap. The construction crew said, "Told you so," but the site supervisor had already called the fire inspectors so we just had to wait. Sure enough, they confirmed our assessment: we failed the inspection.

The next day my uncle gave us kudos for the attempt but even more so for admitting we had failed. He asked us to explain our cement solution to confirm what we really knew. The construction crew had many ideas but all were costly and they would take more than a week. We ran the idea by the fire inspectors who said it sounded feasible. We got the go-ahead to try one more time.

It worked and we got approval from the fire inspector. It was the last inspection needed for the building to open and the site supervisor said to me, "If you hadn't been upfront about your first attempt, we would've turned this over to the construction crew. The fact that you admitted that you screwed up was the main reason you got the second chance."

In business, you want to be the one chosen to solve a customer's problems, especially if you cause them. You want that second chance. The best way to ensure that you get the opportunity to solve a problem is to be the one to identify it. Again, this is not about getting credit or assigning blame, it is about advising. Those who earn the position of trusted advisor will also earn lifelong customers.

Being Dressed Down Can Dress You Up

No matter how well you and your company perform, there will always be a point when the customer is uncomfortable or unhappy about how things are going. They can be unhappy about something specific or they can just be generally nervous about the project. Sometimes, they just need to vent.

With some people, venting can come in the form of complaints, with others it can be an angry rant. When customers are angry or disappointed, oftentimes the critique is unfiltered and can come across as a personal attack. You might hear problems attributed to you that you really have no control over. No matter what you hear, the best thing you can do is to listen. The worst thing you can do is to be defensive and/or try to make excuses.

(Note: There will be time for you to explain the situation, if you can, but the time is not right when the customer is too angry to hear it.)

It is important to remember that decision-makers are betting on you to come through for them. They chose you to help them be successful and when the unexpected happens, it's a natural human emotion to be upset. The benefit is that people often display more of their personality and character when they are angry. When you listen, you not only learn more about their personal motivations but you silently communicate to them that you are accountable and will not wilt under pressure. That is why being dressed down can dress you up.

My First Sales Call on Boeing

I was thirty years old when I made my first sales call on Boeing. I met with an IT director named Al, who managed the support of all computer systems used by Boeing Commercial Airplane Company (BCAC). I made that first call with my manager's manager, Neil. Al purposely kept us waiting in his outer office for quite a while. (It is still standard procedure in many companies to keep "vendors" waiting to emphasize that they are the boss.) Al's assistant finally escorted us into his office where we quickly got through the introductions.

As we were sitting down, Al, who looked like Marlon Brando's character in the movie *The Godfather*, said, "I don't know why you guys are here because as long as I'm in this job HP will never sell another computer here. So, what are you here for?" We had that inevitable uncomfortable silence but then I asked, "Why?" Al was obviously irritated and lit in to a long rant about how he had enough trouble supporting all the IBM and DEC computers in BCAC, and the last time his team managed an HP server the application was "garbage." I would estimate that Al went on for about five minutes, ending his statement asking, "Wanna know more?" He sat there with crossed arms. I said, "Thanks for your frankness." Then we left. In the car Neil said, "This will test you." He chuckled and we drove back to the office.

During the next nine months, I did not sell a single computer to BCAC, but I found customers who needed applications that ran on HP servers. Together we found used HP computers in the Boeing warehouse, which the BCAC groups could get at no cost. Interestingly, each of those systems needed disk drives and terminals in order to operate but those were all expense items and were not capital expenditures. During that nine-month period, BCAC procured and installed sixteen *free* HP computers from their own storage warehouse and I sold over two million dollars of disk drives and terminals. In December of that year, I got a call from Al's assistant saying he wanted to see me immediately.

I went to his office and waited again for quite a while. I finally got permission to enter; I shook hands with Al, and sat down. He sat there with his arms crossed rocking in his big leather chair, just staring at me. I sat there in silence for probably thirty seconds (that felt like thirty minutes) before Al said, "You're a pretty smart guy." (In that Godfather-like tone.) I literally did not know if he was mad, being sarcastic, or both. He went on to say, "So I understand we have sixteen more HP computers we have to support. Is that right?" I said, "Yes." Again, he went silent and just stared at me. I thought it would be my last meeting at Boeing. Instead, Al said, "And I didn't buy any of them, did I?" I told him they all came out of the Boeing Stores.

He went on to say that they would have to hire three more people to support the HP systems and then with a sly smile on his face he said, "So that team loves you right now." He let out a big laugh and went on to say that it was not usually a good thing to out-smart him, but in this case, "You done good."

That same person who told me he would never buy from me became one of my best customers. Al also became such a good lifelong customer that when his son went to work for Microsoft, he asked me to watch out for him. That dressing down certainly dressed me up.

In Summary

By being unreasonably accountable, being predictable, anticipating challenges, communicating bad news, and listening when a customer is angry or unhappy, you create a culture of no surprises. A culture of no surprises earns you RELIABILITY and that will earn lifelong customers for you and your company.

Putting It to Work: Exercises

RELIABILITY – Being there when the unexpected happens, because it always will.

Do decision-makers and influencers know exactly how you would respond if something were to go wrong?   Yes   No

If no:

Have you reviewed and gotten approval for your escalation process?   Yes   No

Do you have current or past failed executions with these decision-makers and/or influencers?   Yes   No

Have you notified your customer of known problems that would negatively surprise decision-makers and/or influencers? Yes   No

Have decision-makers and/or influencers expressed interest and/or issues about you or your company's ability to meet commitments?   Yes   No

For each no, document why you think this is happening.

For each reason why the answer is no, document your best next action for changing it to yes.

CHAPTER 7
PROBLEM SOLVING AND PLANNING

Selling is a series of problem-solving steps on the way to winning and keeping lifelong customers. Whether you are addressing internal or external problems associated with one or more of *The Five Abilities*, you are problem solving. This is the core of what you do as a salesperson; the best salespeople tend to be natural problem solvers because they enjoy helping people. Helping customers by understanding their needs, both business and personal, enables you to create consistently workable solutions for your customers and clients resulting in winning lifelong customers.

Stating the obvious, solving complex problems is hard. However, when we understand the key barriers and follow a common, simple method, we tend to get better ideas that generally lead to better solutions and better participation by all stakeholders. The result is comprehensive and collaborative problem solving. Often when actions fail, it is not the solution that was bad but the execution. Execution fails most often because stakeholders are not on board and/or they are not working on the same solution. Getting everyone on the same page is a big part of making things work.

Barriers to Collaborative Problem Solving

Have you ever been to a meeting meant to solve a problem, and found that open discussion results in closed minds? Have you found that some people come with ready-made answers with reverse-justification that molds the problem to fit their solution? In my earlier story about the delayed tunnel in Seattle, many city leaders started that discussion knowing that the tunnel was the only solution even though they had not yet heard all the proposals. A tunnel was cool. Another road was not.

Alternatively, have you seen the inverse where smart people do not speak up until the meeting is ending, and then they ask a question that nobody can answer? Have you seen people who would rather have their idea chosen than for the group to choose the right idea? You have likely seen all of these situations and you know that these barriers result in a failure to participate in comprehensive and collaborative problem solving, which generally means no problem solving at all.

Conducting business in large and small enterprises requires contributions by many people. There are very few cases when real results come from the work of a single individual, whether the founder, the CEO, or an individual contributor.

Collaborative problem solving has the benefit of surfacing better ideas, but equally important, it also brings all stakeholders together on the way to a single solution. When stakeholders are part of finding the solution, they are more likely to take part in executing it, and in enterprises that can be the difference between success and failure.

To accomplish collaborative problem solving it is important to understand and acknowledge the main things that keep us from being optimally productive.

1. *No Collective Understanding of the Problem*

It is a simple concept and yet many groups fail to take the time to ensure that everyone intends to solve the same problem. Taking the necessary time to develop a collective understanding significantly increases the productivity of even the smallest group.

2. *The Human Desire to Be Right*

No matter how experienced we are at problem solving, individuals still find pleasure in being right. Each of us celebrates differently but we all have emotional and physical responses when we learn we are right. The problem comes when being right is more important than finding the right solution.

3. *One-Third to One-Half of the Population Are Introverts*

In Susan Cain's impactful book, *Quiet: The Power of Introverts in a World That Can't Stop Talking*[6] we learn that introverts actually have something to say. When we take time to listen to them, we often find better ideas. The problem comes when we get in a room full of extroverted debaters and the introverts cannot find a way in.

4. *Start with the Answers and Reverse-Engineer the Problems*

Much more often than we would like to believe, we think we know the answer before discussing and analyzing the problem. We start with our answer and try to reverse-engineer the problem so it fits that answer. This is exactly backwards. How does this happen? Maybe the boss has an answer and nobody is willing to disagree. Maybe the loudest person has an answer and nobody else can out-shout them. We may have a very intelligent solution that makes us look so smart that we conveniently ignore those nasty things called facts.

For whatever reason, human beings are often prone to making assumptions and working the wrong path leading us to choose the seemingly smartest and most complex solutions rather than solutions that just work.

5. *We Address WHAT Is Wrong Rather Than WHY It Is Happening*

The most common mistake in problem solving is to address the symptoms and not the real problem. We do not really understand why we are getting an undesired result and we do not explore the options that address WHY problems are happening.

WHAT – WHY – WHAT – A Problem-Solving Discipline

In finding workable solutions that win business and lifelong customers, you get help from using a simple tool that leads to comprehensive and collaborative solutions. I call this simple tool What-Why-What, which enforces discipline that leads you to answer the following questions:

- WHAT do you see, hear, and/or know that tells you there is a problem?
- WHY are the things that you see, hear, and/or know happening?
- WHAT can you do, that is within your control, to address WHY the problem occurs?

WHAT Do You See, Hear, and/or Know?

First, identify the symptoms that tell you something is wrong. I had a manager who used to say, "Does the patient have a fever?" Deborah, who was a Senior Vice President, wanted to know that we were seeing, hearing, or knowing real things that indicated there was a problem or that there was one coming.

For example, in any business that sells via channel partners or resellers, we constantly have to analyze what we call "sell-in" and "sell-through" revenue. *Sell-in revenue* refers to the amount of product currently held by the channel—what we call channel inventory. *Sell-through revenue* is how much the channel actually sells to end-user companies and/or consumers. If one or both of these numbers are below expectations, we have a problem. In

Deborah's terms, we have a fever. Based on what we see, hear, and know we are able to define what the problem is.

Another example is in manufacturing facilities; they often measure output or yield. For example, how many cars leave the assembly line each day? How many iPhone screens arrive at final assembly each day? If the answer was, "Fewer than expected," then as Deborah would say, "The patient has a fever."

Once we know that the patient has a fever, do we put the patient in an ice bath, do we administer aspirin, or do we just wait and see? A doctor would say, "I don't know. It depends on *WHY* the patient has the fever."

WHY Are the Things We See, Hear, and Know Happening?

Understanding *why* something is happening is the most import-ant step in collaborative problem solving because addressing the why is how we find real solutions. This is how we avoid the dangerous path of reacting to symptoms, which can be expensive and a waste of time. The reason many naturally react to symptoms is because we can see, feel, or experience them, but unfortunately, the symptoms often are only part of the problem. In a medical situation, doctors will treat symptoms to comfort the patient or to keep other problems from arising, but neither cures the malady. The same is true in business—treating symptoms does not lead to real, lasting solutions.

We also can trick ourselves into thinking that any quick reac-tion is better than no reaction at all—even if it does not address the problem. The easiest, quickest thing to do is just to do something even if we do not know why. An added complication is that in many cultures, just doing something—*anything*—no matter the result, earns praise, which causes people to repeat the behavior. We see this a lot in politics when officials get accolades on the evening news, simply for proposing legislation to address symptoms just so they can claim action, even if the solution never results in anything meaningful. Talk big, talk loud, get press, and then blame someone else when nothing works. Fortunately, that only works in politics.

Real problem solving addresses WHY the problem exists and not simply WHAT the symptoms are. Depending on each person's context, why something is happening is always open for debate, but gaining agreement on why a problem exists is the first step to real problem solving.

Addressing a Symptom: Selling Intellectual Property in Asia

In parts of Asia, companies that sell intellectual property have difficulty collecting payment for their products. Software, music, and movies have always been very easy to copy and now even counterfeiting hard goods like iPhones and iPads has become common.

When the industries were tackling this challenge during the first decade of the twenty-first century, there were many who fell back on the original four Ps of marketing (Product, Price, Promotion, and Place) trying to identify the problem. (I know there are many variations ranging from five Ps to seven Ps, but the core four suffice for this example.)

We concluded that we had the right *products* because the organizations that invested in making counterfeit versions only focused on devices and software that were massively popular. We had no lack of brand recognition so our *promotions* seemed to be working fine. Ironically, our products were selling like hotcakes everywhere so *distribution* was not a problem. The challenge was that only a small fraction were genuine products made by the companies who owned the intellectual property. You could buy the latest *Spiderman* movie for three dollars, even though it had not yet launched in theaters. You could buy Office 2010 in the year 2008.

All we had left to consider was *price* and since there is still a large population in Asia living in poverty, most companies assumed that products were too expensive; that people copied and counterfeited our goods because of cost. We took a very common business approach and put everything on sale with the expectation that people would buy them, find out they were great, and buy them again, at full price, after we ended the sale.

Many companies did the same and then a consistent pattern developed. Sales would go up for one or two months following a price decrease, but then unit sales would fall back to where they were before the price decrease. This happened even when we did not raise the price back to the previous levels.

Industries got more scientific by conducting polls and focus groups to find out what companies and consumers would be willing to pay for various IP products. We had all kinds of studies that showed $20 was all we could charge for products that cost $50 everywhere else in the world. Companies started creating special localized products to reduce prices further, only to experience the same result. One or two months of increased sales only to have unit sales return to where they were before.

The problem was that we all started with the answer rather than determining WHY we had the problem. We started with the assumption that price was WHY products did not sell, so our questions led people to search for the answer we wanted—a lower price. Instead of asking, "What would motivate you to pay for XYZ product?" researchers asked, "How much is XYZ product worth to you? $20? $25? $30?" You know what they chose.

Why Would Anyone Pay for Something That Was Free?

Later we went back to ask the other question—what would motivate you to pay full price for XYZ product? The overwhelming answer was "nothing." The vast majority of people were willing to pay exactly zero. When we asked why, the answer was, "Because only stupid people pay for something you can get for free."

After years of research, we came to the realization that price reductions did not result in anything permanent and that the focus had to be on two things: creating value derived from being our customer, and making it harder to copy our products. It is an ongoing battle faced by all companies selling intellectual property, but now we know that our simple assumption about pricing was not the reason WHY people refused to pay for our products.

Starting with the solution is always dangerous because it does not force you to understand WHY a problem exists. If you cannot determine WHY the problem exists, you cannot truly solve the problem. Ask open questions and record whatever you see, hear, and/or know. Finding the WHY in this fashion is the only way you can truly solve problems in a collaborative way.

Just as you would not expect your doctor to prescribe medicine without first knowing WHY you have a fever, you cannot react to a problem before knowing WHY. Taking the time to understand WHY will pay off in the end. Understanding WHY has the same effect as coming up with a great strategy. Once you understand WHY a problem exists, you become more focused and more creative about WHAT you can do. You know WHY your patient has a fever.

WHAT Can You Do That Is Within Your Control, to Address WHY the Problem Occurs?

You develop better solutions when you avoid the bright and shiny, clever ideas that you cannot really do. It is not a workable solution if key elements are outside of your control.

Solutions Outside of Your Control

Let us revisit the counterfeiting issue in Asia. In 2005, we got an opportunity to solve this problem. Leaders in China had decided they wanted better relations with the World Trade Organization (WTO). Prominent members of the WTO including the United States and many other Western nations were home to industries that relied on global support of intellectual property rights (IPR). As stated earlier, among the industries most affected were those that produced movies, music, and software.

Chinese leaders needed to have economic and commercial support from the United States to become WTO members, and in return, the US needed the Chinese government to enforce global IPR laws. In September 2005, there would be a meeting between US President George W. Bush and Chinese President Hu Jintao, in Washington, DC, to discuss these issues.

The meeting between the presidents never took place. Hurricane Katrina, which hit the American Gulf Coast in August 2005, caused President Bush to postpone the meeting. Instead, President Hu attended a summit in Seattle, WA, where then Secretary of State, Condoleezza Rice and leaders from major US companies hosted him and other global officials.

Things Looked Great—for a While

US leaders agreed to give China more support as part of the WTO and China's leaders agreed to enforce IPR regulations. For a period of about nine months, Chinese PC manufacturers and resellers complied with licensing and reselling requirements for software. We had multiple meetings with Chinese CEOs who showed us the IPR decrees they had received from their Ministry of Technology, and for many months, our conversations were about helping them to become compliant.

Reality: We Counted On Things Outside of Our Control

We made what looked to be much progress during those nine months, but unfortunately, in 2006, Chinese leaders began to lose confidence in the WTO. Additionally, the meeting between the presidents went from postponement to a formal cancellation. We learned how little control we truly had over the companies with whom we were doing business in China. In less than a year all the challenges we had before that summit had returned and customers were angry that they had paid more for that short period.

The moral to the story is that the solution created was never within our control. While it was a very bright and shiny path to utilize global relations to achieve our goals, none of us changed our practices to make it more inviting for Chinese customers to do business with us. Worse, Chinese customers never saw the value in paying for genuine products. We did something that looked smart, but in the end, we did not really address WHY Chinese consumers and businesses did not want to pay for our products. Certainly, it was wrong for them to be illegally copying our products, but they didn't see it that way and they no longer got a win by adhering to their own government's mandate.

The movie, music, and software industries are still struggling with this problem. However, in trying to solve it, we learned how things could go terribly wrong when we try to implement solutions that are not truly within our control and that do not address WHY customers did not pay for our products.

You are relying on luck to be successful when choosing to implement solutions that are not within your control. My dad used to say, "Being lucky is great—but it's hard to repeat." He was referring to athletic pursuits, but I have found it applies to business just as well.

When we develop and deploy actions that are within our control, we avoid the foibles that come with relying on luck and realize the success that comes from relying on our ABILITIES.

Scratch-Pad Planning

The best salespeople spend most of their time in front of customers. The best salespeople know the benefits of good planning and reporting, but they also find ways to do it efficiently. To great salespeople, planning is a tool, not an assignment done once a year. It is a means to uncover new and best actions—not simply a means to report what you have already done.

In the beginning of this book I referenced the three-day training and planning sessions where people left asking, "Now what do we do?" I have also been part of training sessions that left us with a much better sense of our strategies and the associated actions. To this day, I still use principles taught to many of us by Nathan Steele, the author of *Strategic Clarity: The Essentials of High-Level Selling.*[7] Nathan taught us to define a strategy for winning, which has been a productive tool for me since I first attended his workshops. Nathan continues to be a friend and mentor.

Nathan's Strategic Clarity model was the standard planning methodology for the OEM Division where I was then a sales manager, and I was able to find complimentary elements between what he taught and how I approached sales with *The Five Abilities*. *The Five Abilities* helped me to answer my team members when they asked, "Now what do we do?" I discovered that when salespeople cannot proceed with their best next action it usually has to do with tactical tuning rather than changing strategy.

The most common example is when salespeople encounter gatekeepers blocking their engagement with decision-makers. After clearly defining their strategy and key tactics, they still are unable to get to decision-makers because they cannot get past the gatekeepers. I found that salespeople often forget that gatekeepers make business decisions for personal reasons too, and that they are often key influencers to decision-makers. This simply means that you must invest tactical energy in delivering value to gatekeepers.

With this in mind, I developed a very simple template to help my team members quickly identify and execute on the best next actions, whether with decision-makers or gatekeepers. The template below helps you uncover best next actions in thirty minutes or less. It will unblock your thinking and lead you, with confidence, to your best next actions.

(**Note about gatekeepers**: People who act as gatekeepers will often challenge your tactics, not because they want to be pests but because they also need to deliver value to decision-makers. Gatekeepers win when they open the door for salespeople who deliver value. They lose when they let someone through who has no value to offer. When gatekeepers challenge you, it comes from the decision-maker challenging them. Listen to them, sell to them, help them win, and you will win.)

Tactics Change Often—Strategies Do Not

Years ago, my peer, Julie, had a customer whose chief goal was to expand their business into China. We determined that our strategy was to convince the customer's new president, Brett, that we were the best positioned to get them placed with the largest resellers in China. We built a solid proposal that our team presented to the customer's executives in Asia, most of whom gave us very positive feedback. Unfortunately, we were unsuccessful in getting an audience with Brett. He told his team, "What they're proposing is just more of the same."

Brett had been in his role for less than a year and his previous company was our chief competitor. We learned from people with whom we had strong relationships that when they presented him with our proposal he, in turn, presented them with his former employer's proposal. We also learned that Brett's assistant and business manager had instructions not to schedule meetings with us. We had a perplexing situation caused by the personal reasons that were motivating Brett's business decision. Without being able to sell to Brett, we could not execute our strategy.

Our executives argued with Julie, saying we had the wrong strategy; that we needed to change our strategy by selling directly to Brett's boss, their CEO. They wanted Julie to go around Brett. Julie knew that in the long-term, as Brett gained more credibility and control, we would put the rest of our significant business with that company at risk. Julie's strategy to convince Brett was correct and we just had to find different tactics to get to him.

In this case, we had a strong relationship with a senior manager Jim, who had also worked for the same competitor and who knew Brett well. Jim was not involved in China, but Julie met with him to discuss our proposal. Jim suspected we had value that Brett needed to see in order to make a sound decision. Through Jim, Julie was able to book a fifteen-minute meeting with Brett.

That fifteen-minute meeting turned into an hour and fifteen minutes because Brett suspected the same value as Jim. That meeting led Julie to a series of discussions with people she had not met, but who had influence on the decision. In the end, Julie won that business. She stuck to her strategy but found different tactics to be visible, credible, viable, capable, and reliable to the right people, in the right way, at the right time.

Tactical Adjustments Come Often and Come Quickly

I have witnessed and experienced many situations like this where we have to change our tactics, on the spot, in order to find new best next actions that win us VISABILITY, CREDABILITY, VIABILITY, CAPABILITY, and RELIABILITY. I created a very simple tool that will help you to identify your problems, quickly, and determine your new best next actions to address them.

The Five Abilities® Action Matrix (What/Why/What)

	VISABILITY Are DM's & I's asking to meet with you?	CREDABILITY Are DM's & I's asking for advice beyond products/services you deliver?	VIABILITY Are discussions primarily focused on results and, specifically not on costs?	CAPABILITY Do you know DM's & I's personal motivations for buying?	RELIABILITY Have DM's & I's stopped asking "What happens when something goes wrong?"
Yes or No?					
What do you see, hear & know that's problematic?					
Why is it happening?					
What can we do, within our control, to address the Why?					

DM – Decision Maker   I - Influencer

THE FIVE ABILITIES®

In Summary

Solving complex problems and doing it in a collaborative way is hard but necessary. Using the What-Why-What tool takes you on a logical path to problem resolution that does not just address the symptoms but instead addresses WHY you have the problem.

Addressing the WHY with actions that are within your control leads you to design permanent solutions for your customers. Avoiding the expensive and often failed path of addressing assumptions also makes you more capable and reliable for your customers. Using the Scratch-Pad Planning tool leads you to follow the What-Why-What discipline while also giving you a working tool that allows quick, productive tuning of your best next actions.

Putting It to Work: Exercises

Planning your best next actions. Go back to the exercises in Chapters 2 through 6, and record the actions you identified for each corresponding **ABILITY**.

VISABILITY: Best next actions (from Chapter 2) with the target date for completion.

1.

2.

3.

4.

CREDABILITY: Best next actions (from Chapter 3) with the target date for completion.

1.

2.

3.

4.

VIABILITY: Best next actions (from Chapter 4) with the target date for completion.

1.

2.

3.

4.

CAPABILITY: Best next actions (from Chapter 5) with the target date for completion.

1.

2.

3.

4.

RELIABILITY: Best next actions (from Chapter 6) with the target date for completion.

1.

2.

3.

4.

CHAPTER 8

KEY TRAITS
OF SALESPEOPLE WHO
WIN LIFELONG CUSTOMERS

How to hire and motivate salespeople is a common debate among sales managers and compensation specialists. A typical assumption is that money drives salespeople so much that all we need to do is pay more to make them perform. That money-driven motivation also shapes hiring practices with the assumption that big signing bonuses and high commission rates will naturally attract the best.

While there are salespeople who feed this stereotype, if we assume the love of money is the sole—or even main—driver of great salespeople, we would not only be wrong, we'd miss the truly effective ways to motivate salespeople and to get the best out of them. In more than thirty years in sales, sales management, and executive management, I have worked with thousands of sales professionals and *not one* that was consistently a top performer, and mentor to others, counted income as their key motivator.

Certainly, salespeople want higher incomes to provide more for their families and communities, just as any professional. I work with professionals in medicine, social services, education, and even religion—all who want to make and/or raise more money. However, not one who is consistently successful, including salespeople, counts money as a top motivator; rather, they see money as a metric and a tool. Good doctors see increased revenue as an indicator that they are providing good service. Good church leaders see increased donations as a sign that they are providing meaningful support for people. In reality, salespeople succeed by how much they increase market share and profit. How much they earn is not always an indicator, since market conditions can result in "bluebirds" or business that arrives by pure luck.

I serve on the board of directors of a Christian nonprofit organization that provides transitional housing to homeless families with children. The motivation for everyone in the organization is to provide housing and services that help the homeless transition from homelessness to independence. However, one way we necessarily determine whether we are reaching the right people with the right messages is by how much money we can raise each year.

Are we growing our fundraising faster than our costs of running the operation? Are we broadening the number of donors? Are we raising enough money to add new programs that increase our success rates of graduating the homeless to independence? Are we helping more people? The competition, if you will, is to serve the homeless in the best ways possible and part of the score is in dollars.

It is the same with salespeople—in particular those who are best at winning lifelong customers. In general, the business scorecard is about revenue, costs, and profits. For salespeople on the frontline as the primary customer-facing function, exceeding volume and revenue targets is job one. In all industries, exceeding targets results in salespeople making more money, and in many companies, the sales role is one of the highest paid professions already, which all leads to the money-hungry stereotype.

As I said before, that would be wrong. Money is a way to keep score, but the true motivators are the *joy of winning*, the *joy of helping*, and the *joy of relating*.

Joy of Winning

The best salespeople are addicted to competing and winning. That characteristic drives them to be in constant search for the extra action to increase their probability of winning. The best salespeople work hard because they practice productive paranoia that comes from being ultra-competitive, not because they starve for the big payday. They simply want to win and they know that if they ease up, the competition will pass them by.

Great salespeople also know how to learn when they do not win. They clearly distinguish between losing and getting beat. Losing is the hardest to take because it means they didn't do all they could and realized it too late. Something either got by them or they just failed to work hard enough to win. On the other hand, being beat happens when they did everything within their control and still lost. Sometimes the competition is just better. (It would be like me going one-on-one with LeBron James. It would be a miracle if I got off a single shot. *He is just that good!*)

The best salespeople learn from both losing and getting beat so that they do not repeat the same mistakes. They gain strategic knowledge that helps them understand who they should be competing with and who they should not. In every sales situation, you learn to be better for the next competition.

How to Spot Competitive Salespeople

Is there something we can look for to ensure we are hiring people who are addicted to competing and winning? In a *Harvard Business Review* article titled, "What Separates the Strongest

Salespeople from the Weakest?"[8] they found that over eighty-five percent of top salespeople played an individual or team sport in high school. The article points out that people who specifically choose to play sports tend to do better in sales. It didn't matter if the athlete was a star or not. What mattered is that they chose to compete.

I have witnessed this personally and in my experience, it applies to all competitive pursuits, not just athletics. A few years ago, I had the opportunity to be at a dinner hosted by Fujitsu in Munich, Germany, where the guest speaker was the famed chess champion Garry Kasparov. Seated at the head table with him, I heard how he related chess to his business pursuits. I expected him to talk about how chess taught him strategy, but the first thing he said was that chess taught him how to compete. He talked about practice, improving his mental toughness, and about how the game started before he sat down at the board.

I have observed the connection between sports and sales success for many years and now we have supporting research. What are things that we learn from competitive activities that make for great salespeople?

- **Learning from winning, losing, and getting beat.** No matter what the outcome, you learn things that make you more unbeatable the next time. You learn by getting beat by a better team. You learn equally as much by losing when you fail to prepare well.
- **Collaborating with a diverse set of people.** Whether playing individual or team sports, you quickly learn that disagreement with teammates must not interfere with your effort. You might have teammates you don't like, but when taking the field you must collaborate to win. Athletes tend to be good at staying focused on the bigger picture.
- **Practice.** Sports teach you how to develop great habits. In sales, the more you do the right things, the better you will get. The more you practice building and

delivering compelling value propositions, the more it becomes habit. The more you successfully deal with rejection, the easier it becomes. Turning hard things into habit is a major difference between great and average salespeople.

- **Getting on board even if you disagree.** You will not always agree with the play calls. Even so, everyone has to perform his or her role in order for the team to win. I was a running back and I wanted the ball to a fault. I would get angry when I did not get the ball. I found myself on the bench until Coach Jim Wilkin (who played for Oregon State University 1964-66) showed me a film of my missed blocks on pass plays. He said, "You're the best ball carrier we have but if you don't block you won't play." He helped me make blocking a habit and I became a starter again.

Certainly, sports are not the only indicator of future success for salespeople and sales managers, but now we have research that shows there is a relationship between the two. Whether they were bit players, starters, or stars, the research says that they have the foundation to be successful in sales and sales management.

Joy of Helping

Great salespeople like to help others. Whether it is delivering information on your product or spending time with an associate who sustained injuries in a car accident, great salespeople have a need to be helpful. I was at Hewlett-Packard when "The HP Way" was still paramount—back when Packard's garage became the birthplace of the Silicon Valley.

Many things went into the HP culture that Bill Hewlett and Dave Packard created, but most of this successful business culture focused on the ways people treated each other. Dave Packard taught us all to "treat everyone like a customer" because someday you might need their help and you are better off if they want to help you.

That culture was so successful that it was part of business school curriculums on how to manage and lead. We learned by example from Bill and Dave but also from Lew Platt, another icon of Silicon Valley (part of California State Route 87 was named for him as a memorial). Before becoming CEO of HP, Lew was the assigned executive for the Boeing relationship. He visited Seattle quarterly for many years, so those of us on the Boeing team had the fortune of getting to know him.

Lew not only promoted the culture but he lived it. Whether you were the GM who ran the Pacific Northwest, a sales manager, salesperson, or a server in the cafeteria, Lew treated you like a customer. You knew he was interested in helping you, no matter who you were—he embodied The HP Way. That along with his incredible business acumen and leadership skills led him into the CEO's suite, got him appointed as President Bill Clinton's Chairman of the World Trade Organization Taskforce, and it made him a very impactful Board Chairman of the Boeing Corporation.

The list of accolades and achievements goes on for Lew, but one thing we all got to experience was that he was an incredible salesperson. He was great to have on sales calls because he was genuinely interested in helping customers and helping us. He did not always agree with our customers or us but no matter what, you knew he was listening to you. He engaged us, and our customers, with the clear purpose of helping to find solutions that would result in winning business, and more importantly, winning lifelong customers.

Joy of Relating

Great salespeople relate well to a diverse set of people. They are genuinely interested in the knowledge they gain from relating well with and to others. It is more common than most think for salespeople to be introverted, but still be very curious about what they can learn from others and how they can help them.

It is also important to note that introversion is not necessarily synonymous with shyness. The joy of relating comes from the person's desire to obtain knowledge from other people rather than from a book, film, or other means.

The best salespeople are not necessarily stereotypical, smooth-talking, cutthroat, aggressive, big personalities. They are not always the people that close the hardest during the interview, and in fact, many great salespeople will tell you they do not use the hard close. They also are not the people who network in the stereotypical ways; not everyone can walk into a room and become the life of the party.

Relating Through Networking

Search for "networking" on Amazon and you will find over 250,000 books. Bing gets you 23 million results and Google gets you a whopping 500+ million hits. It is a popular topic of books and blogs, and while some hits apply to computer networking, many apply to the act of making beneficial connections with other people.

In business, generally, and sales specifically, one has to be a great networker to be successful. With salespeople and sales leaders, we have to hire the Rolodex™ *builder,* not just the Rolodex.[9] You absolutely want salespeople who connect well with a diverse set of people so they can create new and varied sales opportunities. Moreover, as mentioned above, you do not have to be an extrovert to have great networking skills. I know this from personal experience.

My uncle took me to Kiwanis Club meetings when I was a teenager. He wanted me to learn how to make a "good first impression." A strong handshake, a confident introduction, look people square in the eyes, and "make small talk." I would observe others in the room who were truly enjoying the small talk, but while I would try, I just was not good at it. Even so, I would never fail to find adults who wanted to have a deeper conversation, resulting in great exchanges about everything from sports to what to study in college.

Following college graduation, I mentioned that my first job was selling checks to financial institutions, and one of my early responsibilities was to do booth duty at financial industry trade shows. My job was to "work the booth," but I also had to attend the cocktail hours and hand out at least fifty business cards: a strong handshake, a confident introduction, look people square in the eyes, and "make small talk." The thing I hated so much was now my job. How did that happen?

Just as I did at the Kiwanis Club meetings, I found people who were not interested in small talk but instead wanted deeper conversations. Sometimes we talked business, but often we dove into other topics and the people I met were happy to have deeper conversations. Like me, they did not relish the act of mingling.

I learned many things from why hay bales are round, to the surprises one finds while hiking the Pacific Crest Trail. I had a long conversation with a Miss America contestant who shared with me how it felt not making the top ten and how the experience affected her career in banking. These same people wanted to learn about me in return and we found a genuine desire to meet after the event. I failed miserably at handing out business cards, but I excelled at getting first meetings that turned into business.

During my early days at Microsoft, I took a management training class that included an abbreviated version of the Myers-Briggs personality test. Not surprisingly, I tested as an introvert, which shocked the instructor since I had just become a Director of Sales. He suggested that my test results were wrong and said, "There's no way you could have succeeded in sales as an introvert." The *assumption* was that all salespeople are extroverts.

Most people would probably make the same assumption as that instructor, but in Susan Cain's book *Quiet: The Power of Introverts in a World That Can't Stop Talking*[10], we learn that almost fifty percent of the population is introverted. This means there is a high probability that many successful salespeople are introverted but are still great networkers. What are the best networking skills of introverts?

- **Listening**: Introverts are naturally good listeners because they dislike monopolizing the conversation. Not surprisingly, customers like salespeople who listen well.
- **Accountability and conflict avoidance**: Per Cain's research, introverts are naturally introspective. In my observations, when the unexpected happens it is more natural for introverted people to ask first, "What could I have done differently?" They prefer to problem-solve before speaking out. Casting unwarranted blame causes conflict so introverts avoid it—when there is disagreement, it happens in a respectful fashion. People buy from accountable problem solvers.
- **Reserved**: One of the negative stereotypes of salespeople is that we are loud, big personalities who are insincere and money-hungry. The movie *Tin Men*[11] depicts the stereotype well. However, I have heard from many customers that my reserved personality eliminates the stereotypical views and puts them at ease.

If you grew up in the United States or other Western cultures, you likely learned to equate extroverted personalities with traits of success, but today's research finds many examples of successful introverts such as Bill Gates, Warren Buffett, J. K. Rowling, and Richard Branson; the list goes on.

Being a great networker and salesperson does not hinge on whether you are an extrovert or an introvert. It hinges on your ability to receive and deliver interesting and relevant knowledge. Listening, accountability, and an inviting personality are some of the best networking skills of both introverts and the salespeople whom we consistently see winning lifelong customers.

The Makings of a Great Sales Leader

Most business leaders believe that, at minimum, sales managers and directors must have sales experience. Furthermore, most hiring executives require that prospective sales leaders have successful sales experience in the industry for which they are hiring. "Selling experience within the industry to which you apply was requested by seventy-two percent of listings," says Jay Ivey, a market research associate at Software Advice, a website that offers sales-enablement software comparisons.

Additionally, we have to look for salespeople who are clear about how they work and why they have been successful. It is this awareness that allows them to be good coaches, strategists, and the best sales leaders. "What makes top sales performers different from the rest is that they know why they win and can repeat it," says Irene Bjorklund, who was Northwest Area General Manager at Hewlett-Packard when I worked there.

Bjorklund is now President of T-Bar Construction and says, "Some salespeople succeed for a while by utilizing their knowledge, relationships, timing, and luck, but the people who are consistently top performers know how to win repeatedly." Great sales people act purposefully and do not rely on luck.

To repeat my dad's advice, "Luck is great, but it's hard to repeat." What traits do we look for?

Purpose and Precision

The best sales professionals engage in each sales situation having researched the situation so that they progress with a clear purpose, one that leads them to precise actions. This clarity allows them to repeat success, and more importantly, it allows them to teach others, which makes them successful leaders. When looking for sales leaders, ask people how they succeed and what they do consistently well in every sales situation. The ones who make great sales leaders are very clear on how they've been successful such that you know they can repeat it. They can also coach others how to be successful which is what you need from great sales managers.

Leadership Experience

You are looking for people who can guide teams to be cohesive, collaborative, and consistently productive with both co-workers and customers. However, this does not necessarily mean the candidate needs formal sales management experience.

One reason management experience is less of a requirement is that leadership skills come by means other than management roles. Leadership skills come from sports, military, community, other management roles, etc. Therefore, while a history of success managing in your industry is nice to have, look for other leadership experiences that salespeople may have had outside the business world.

Ask manager candidates what they look for in people they hire. An important trait is to find leaders who know their weaknesses and are comfortable managing people who fill in their holes. Hiring and managing strong people is a consistent trait of great leaders.

Flexible Relationship Skills

Having flexible relationship skills is a common trait of great salespeople and sales leaders. They develop deep, genuine relationships with a diverse set of people. You will see examples through their interactions in both the work environment and their social circles. The key is that their approach to relationships is genuine; they do not build diverse relationships to advance an agenda. They build diverse relationships because they enjoy learning different perspectives. When you find salespeople who have strong, genuine relationships with a wide range of people, you have found someone with a key trait to be successful in sales leadership.

Find salespeople who act with purpose and precision, have successful leadership experience, and display flexible relationship skills, and you will have found people who have the potential to be successful sales leaders for your organization.

Creativity and Improvisation

While this is the end of this chapter, these are very important characteristics for you to find when hiring new team members.

The Pareto principle, or the "80/20 Rule," applies to many professions. It says that about 80 percent of the results come from 20 percent of the effort. This principle applies to opportunity management in that 80 percent of our sales come from 20 percent of our opportunities. It also applies to the sales activity we undertake to win each opportunity since 80 percent of what salespeople deliver is common to all salespeople. The improvisational 20 percent is the unique value that wins 80 percent of the business *and* lifelong customers.

I spent seven years trying to make it in the music industry where the 80/20 rule also applies. Eighty percent is what everyone plays: the melodies, chords, and rhythms. All musicians must do it and many get by just doing that 80 percent well. However, unique creativity and improvisation is the 20 percent that makes a musician special enough to win recording contracts and Grammy awards.

To achieve that 20 percent, musicians need to know and practice the melodies, chords, and rhythms enough for them to become habit. When the 80 percent becomes habit, we free up our minds to apply more of our musical abilities to improvisation. Great musicians still follow the same melodies, chords, and rhythms that the rest of us do, but they create and improvise that little bit "extra" that turns cover acts into concert acts.

Sales is very much like playing music; 80 percent of what we must deliver to win business is the same as what our competitors do—the melodies, chords, and rhythms. We all do consistent things to be visible, credible, viable, capable, and reliable. The improvisational 20 percent comes from combining our offers with the customer's needs to create value that is unique to the customer.

It does not mean we change the product, just as great musicians do not change the song. Instead, it means that we might choose to emphasize benefits and talk about them in the customer's language rather than taking a "canned" approach. We become the concert act while our competitors are still playing covers.

In Summary

Hiring, teaching, and retaining salespeople and sales managers who are adept at winning lifelong customers is a priority for all companies. Look for people who are addicted to competing and winning, who thrive when helping others, and who truly enjoy relating to a diverse set of people, and you will find those who have a high likelihood of being the kind of salespeople who make a habit of winning lifelong customers.

CHAPTER 9

SOCIAL MEDIA AND SELLING
HOW IS YOUR JOB DIFFERENT?

Social media and the broader digital age have made access to all information extremely simple. When customers want to know about you, your company, and your product, they simply type in search criteria and they can learn things about you that would have required a private detective just twenty years ago.

The ease of access to product or service information means face-to-face time with customers has to be even more meaningful and at a personal level. When discussing the elements of *The Five Abilities* with business leaders, it's clear that much focus is on using digital communications and social media to create VISABILITY, CREDABILITY and VIABILITY. These methods are necessary if you want your information accessible to today's business decision-makers.

However, in B2B selling, the enhanced ability to share information with your target audience accentuates the need for direct selling. Because product information is so readily available online, the time you get with decision-makers must satisfy the personal side of decision-making. As great sales professionals know, this is the most complex part of the sales process. This does not mean you can forgo in-depth knowledge of your products but instead that you must be able to personalize it to each customer.

I have seen too many salespeople, including myself, take the easy route by pulling out a PowerPoint deck to deluge decision-makers with features and benefits. There was a time when that was the best way for decision-makers to get necessary product information, but that time has passed. Now, more than ever, direct selling is about the decisions you are asking *people* to make, not companies, and your time in front of customers must focus on addressing the personal reasons they should choose you.

Front-Line Accountability

Salespeople have always had front-line accountability for knowing the motivations of decision-makers and other influential people. You are the connection to the company. In today's digital age, the importance of you understanding a decision-maker's personal motivations is greater because the personal connection is one thing for which no algorithm exists. You cannot learn what drives individual decision-makers online and they cannot fully assess a trusted advisor by reading their LinkedIn page. Even with the great advancements in communication technology, we still build trust and confidence through personal interaction.

My Experience

This experience will be familiar to many readers. We were on the verge of a major product launch and I was having dinner with the number-two person at one of the largest companies in the world. He had to decide how much resource his company would invest in working with us, versus our competitor. My team had scheduled the meeting because they were having difficulty convincing this customer to commit to our new offering.

We were having a very pleasant discussion about industry events when the third course arrived, causing a natural break in our discussion. After the server left, the senior executive leaned across the table and said, "Rick, I want to discuss a very difficult decision I have to make." I leaned forward and said "Sure." He said, "For many years we've bet on your company and now I find myself unsure if I can still do that. Can you convince me that I should continue to bet on you?"

Honestly, my team probably remembers my verbal response better than I do, but my words were not the important message. The customer wanted to see my physical reaction. He wanted to see if I was confident that his company would be OK if he chose us. Months later, I saw the same executive and he confirmed to me that he was looking more for the right body language than the right words. We got his business, and it would not have happened on Facebook or Twitter.

Social Media and *The Five Abilities*
VISABILITY

On the one hand, we have so many ways to be visible today compared to when I first started selling in the 1980s. Back then, digital referred to music CDs and social was something you did at parties. On the other hand, too much of anything can be hard to manage and that is true for digital communications and social media.

It is fun to post on Facebook, Instagram, Pinterest, etc. So quick to tweet, Snapchat, WhatsApp, email, etc. So easy to build a profile on LinkedIn or a website on WordPress, WIX, etc. Social media experts can get you started in minutes. Unfortunately, simpler tools have led to more content and your audience tunes out all but the best executions. If you do not have great content and a compelling value proposition, you will not earn VISABILITY with the right people, in the right way, at the right time.

My recommendation is to hire an experienced digital/social marketing consultant who will keep you current on the latest trends. I recommend a book called *Navigating the Talent Shift* by Lisa Hufford[12] that talks about the benefits found in today's on-demand workforce. I recommend taking this path even if you have a dedicated social media team because it allows you and your people to get up-to-date information on an important tool that is perpetually evolving.

CREDABILITY

You earn CREDABILITY when you demonstrate your expertise, educate customers and clients, and advocate for yourself, peers, and partners who can help your prospective buyers. You can do a lot in all three of these things via digital communications and social media. If you are not utilizing these tools, you are behind.

More specifically, if you do not have a website, a completed LinkedIn profile, and if you are not tweeting and "Facebooking" about your expertise, you are not doing the minimum amount of work to earn CREDABILITY in today's business environment. In fact, if you want to be an advisor in addition to being a seller, you likely need to be blogging to earn CREDABILITY in your area of expertise. A good rule of thumb: Sharing content is good; creating content is better; creating heavily shared content is best.

As I emphasize throughout this book, personal connection with decision-makers and influencers is still necessary to be a successful enterprise seller, but getting into the C-Suite is far more challenging today than ever before. The people supporting decision-makers and influencers know almost everything about your product, service, and even you, before the first meeting. If they cannot find the information they need online, your CREDABILITY suffers, and you may never get the appointment you need. You still must be credible in person but you will not get that chance without having a good digital/social presence.

Again, I highly recommend hiring expert consultants even if you have your own marketing team assigned to this challenge, due to the constant changes in this field. For instance, Google search algorithms change regularly and without warning. That alone is justification to have on-demand specialists who can ensure that your teams are posting information that will generate that all-important suspicion-of-value that motivates decision-makers to demand your presence, and ultimately your products and services.

VIABILITY

You confirm VIABILITY by ensuring:

- That the customer/client has **NEED** for your offering.
- That they have the **EXPERIENCE** necessary to evaluate your performance.
- That their **SUCCESS** makes them attractive to your competitors.
- That they have the **TIME** to be successful with your product and/or service.

You must confirm that your offering is viable for your customer but also that the customer is viable for you. The only thing worse than no customer is the wrong customer, and it is largely up to the salesperson to determine the viability of a customer or client.

When prospective customers express a suspicion-of-value about your offering, they are starting the process of confirming, for themselves, that they have NEED for your product or service. It's very hard for content on websites or social media to provide enough diverse kinds of information necessary to address specific concerns for every prospective decision-maker. Most often, the best you can do is to create that suspicion-of-value such that they ask to learn more from you.

You begin to develop confidence in your customer's EXPERIENCE by researching what they do, how they do it, and the results they have created. However, once again, digital and social content rarely gives you enough information to know, with certainty, that the people with whom you will collaborate have the EXPERIENCE and expertise necessary to assess your work.

Assessing a prospective customer's SUCCESS is something you can evaluate by researching digital and social content. However, in very large companies a good corporate profile does not mean that the people with whom you will work are successful within their own ranks. Complete confirmation still takes personal interaction.

Understanding if a customer has enough TIME to be successful is something you can only learn through personal interaction. Even when working with a company that publicizes their deadlines, you cannot understand the internal resource and political contingencies that affect their timelines without talking with project managers and their experts.

You can and should learn all you can about your customer in the areas of Need, Experience, Success, and Time, via online tools. Unfortunately, there is not enough current detail to assess a customer's VIABILITY, nor can they satisfy their questions about you, without personal engagement with decision-makers, influencers, and the people with whom you will be working. We may see innovations in digital communication, security, and access that resolve this, but we are many years away from the efficiency and effectiveness of personal interaction as it regards enterprise selling.

CAPABILITY

It will be a long time before we have technology that accurately tells us a decision-maker's personal motivation for buying. Whether their inspiration comes from Safety, Simplicity, Rewards, Recognition, or Revolution is something you can only learn by engaging with the people who make decisions and those around them. This is one ability, within *The Five Abilities*, that most reaffirms the old adage that "people buy from people."

RELIABILITY

Your customers can see feedback and reviews on almost any product sold simply by doing a Google search on the name of a company's product reviews. What your customer cannot fully learn is what it will be like to work with you and your peers.

People learn about what it's like to work with you by watching how you sell to them. Are you responsive? Are you empathetic? Do you truly understand their problems? Can you influence the decision-makers within your own company should your customer need more than a standard offer? The list of traits that people want to know about you is endless but what they want to know is simple. People want to know that they can rely on you, work with you, and have fun with you. People make business decisions for personal reasons.

In Summary

Earlier in this book, I talked about a very large contract HP received from Boeing. The decision-makers on that project have since retired but I still see them via the old-fashioned social media—parties. Over the years they've shared their decision-making criteria, and in the end, that they decided to buy from us simply because they and their people wanted to work with us. The competitive proposals were not significantly different so it was really all about the people. Again, affirmation that people still buy from people.

In B2B, where a buying decision has large impact, affects many people, and involves significant financial investments, people will have both business and personal motivations driving their decisions. Digital communications and social media help them learn about you and your company, but they will not be comfortable making a buying decision without knowing the people with whom they will work.

There is no doubt that technological innovation has changed the tools we use to sell successfully. Learn to use digital and social to your advantage but for the time being, even with all that innovation, you must still personally sell yourself in order to win lifelong customers.

CHAPTER 10
THE BEST SALE OF MY LIFE

What do these things have in common?

- Asking that special someone for a first date
- Inviting a friend to join you on that dream, cross-country bicycle ride
- Getting investors to take interest in your new venture
- Helping a student buy the right PC for college
- Motivating a CEO to be interested in learning more about your product

In all cases, we are convincing another human being to do something they might not otherwise do. As Daniel Pink says in his bestselling book *To Sell Is Human,*[13] we are constantly trying to, "… coax others to part with resources." We are asking people to spend time, effort, or money that they might not have otherwise spent. Whether you are a salesperson, CEO, or a student, you sell every day.

Learning Brings Earning

You are approaching people to *learn* what would entice them to do what you are asking of them: to help you help them. You are earning VISABILITY that makes you more memorable than others competing for that person's time. You earn CREDABILITY when you demonstrate, educate, and advocate in unique ways that benefit them. When you are more visible and credible you earn VIABILITY over others vying for your subject's attention. You are giving them confidence that all of their expectations will be realized because your CAPABILITY allows you to best address their personal reasons for making business decisions. Lastly, you show up when the unexpected happens, which earns you RELIABILITY in the eyes of the person from whom you are asking for help. You are selling and you do it every day of your life.

In the B2B and B2C worlds, I define selling as *the act of helping people to buy something that benefits them and/or their businesses, within the bounds of what the seller can successfully deliver.*

In our day-to-day personal lives, I define selling as *the act of helping people to do something that benefits them, within the bounds of what we can make happen.*

The point is that these things are not that different. Selling is, above all, a personal act that motivates people to be comfortable with the voluminous data and information that is ever more easily available.

The Ultimate Sale

To pay for college I played in bands and worked in the student cafeteria. I had just transferred to Oregon State University after a brief stint at UCLA. It was the first day of winter term and the cafeteria manager was holding her obligatory all-hands meeting to welcome the student employees. She also introduced her new assistant manager who was responsible for managing all student workers.

The assistant manager was pretty, bubbly, confident, and had an infectious laugh. I knew instantly that I needed to convince her to go out with me; however, there were many challenges ahead. She was two levels above me and I was just one of the 100+ students who worked for her. At the time, she was dating other guys, including a university executive who could afford much fancier dates than a poor, guitar-toting, college student who dreamed of being a recording artist. However, when the assistant manager finished her introduction, she ended by saying, "Let me know if you have any questions." I took her up on that.

I knew she liked to laugh so I would point out funny things happening in the cafeteria and around campus. I also was naturally a hard worker and that left her with a good impression. I was slowly becoming visible and credible to her while at the same time showing her that I was capable of satisfying her personal needs as a manager, and I proved to be a reliable person. My remaining challenge was to create viable reasons as to why she would want to date this younger student rather than the university executive.

As she came to know me better, she told me about how her dates would go. They would do the traditional dinners and movies, which she liked, but she was also into music and sports, things for which her dates showed little interest. How convenient: since I was into sports and music, our conversations began to turn to those topics. I possessed the capabilities that satisfied her personal motivations and she found it viable to date me rather than the university executive.

After two months of creating **VISABILITY** and proving my **CREDABILITY**, **VIABILITY**, **CAPABILITY**, and **RELIABILITY**, I asked, "So when do I get to see you outside of this cafeteria?"

What was the result? I have been married to that pretty, confident, bubbly woman, with the infectious laugh, since 1981.

The best sale I ever made.

In Summary

Businesses do not make decisions—people do, and people make business decisions for personal reasons. Executing on *The Five Abilities* focuses your actions on the personal reasons that lead decision-makers to choose you over your competition. This does not eliminate the need for data and information that helps us make the right business decisions, but the personal element is how you win lifelong customers—the lifeblood of enterprise selling.

As Daniel Pink says, "To sell is human," and you will be more successful in sales, business, and life by continually honing the human deliverables that decision-makers look for when choosing from whom they will buy and for whom they will choose to be a lifelong customer.

Executing *The Five Abilities* sales framework will help you quickly identify your best next actions, with the right combination of business and personal focus, which will significantly increase your sales productivity. Take these lessons to heart, and get out there and sell. (With heart!)

END NOTES

1) *Job Hopping Is the 'New Normal' for Millennials* by Jeanne Meister, August 14, 2012 http://www.forbes.com/sites/jeannemeister/2012/08/14/job-hopping-is-the-new-normal-for-millennials-three-ways-to-prevent-a-human-resource-nightmare/#314189055085

2) *15 Statistics That Should Change the Business World—But Haven't* by Colin Shaw, June 4, 2013 https://www.linkedin.com/pulse/20130604134550-284615-15-statistics-that-should-change-the-business-world-but-haven-t

3) *More money needed for Seattle's delayed tunnel project* by Chris Grygiel (AP), July 21, 2016 http://www.readingeagle.com/apps/pbcs.dll/article?AID=/20160721/AP/307219238/1054

4) *The Devil Wears Prada* (2006) http://www.imdb.com/title/tt0458352/

5) *NCIS* – Television crime drama http://www.imdb.com/title/tt0364845/?ref_=nv_sr_1

6) *Quiet: The Power of Introverts in a World That Can't Stop Talking* by Susan Cain http://www.quietrev.com/team/susan-cain/

7) *Strategic Clarity: The Essentials of High-Level Selling* by Nathan Steele https://www.amazon.com/Strategic-Clarity-Essentials-High-Level-Selling/dp/0972037608/ref=sr_1_1?ie=UTF8&qid=1475010182&sr=8-1&keywords=Strategic+Clarity

8) *What Separates the Strongest Salespeople from the Weakest* by Steve W. Martin, March 18, 2015, Harvard Business Review https://hbr.org/2015/03/what-separates-the-strongest-salespeople-from-the-weakest

9) Rolodex™ is one of the original manual contact management systems and is still used today by many businesses http://www.rolodex.com/products/contact-management

10) *So Begins a Quiet Revolution of the 50 Percent* by Jenna Goudreau, January 30, 2012 – Article about Susan Cain's findings in her book *Quiet: The Power of Introverts in a World That Can't Stop Talking.* http://www.forbes.com/sites/jennagoudreau/2012/01/30/quiet-revolution-of-the-50-percent-introverts-susan-cain/

11) *Tin Men* (1987) – Movie http://www.imdb.com/title/tt0094155/plotsummary

12) *Navigating the Talent Shift* by Lisa Hufford, CEO/Founder Simplicity Consulting www.simplicityci.com

13) *To Sell is Human* by Daniel Pink http://www.danpink.com/books/

INDEX

Rick Wong is the creator of The Five Abilities® sales framework and the founder and CEO of The Five Abilities LLC, a sales consulting firm. Rick has spent more than 35 years growing revenue for Fortune 100 companies as an employee, partner, and seller. He held posts at American Bank Stationery, Hewlett-Packard, and Microsoft, and exited as VP Global Device Partners, in Microsoft's OEM Division. He spent a decade in global leadership roles including three years as VP of Asia for Microsoft's OEM Division and another four years as VP of the group that helped Microsoft's Asian partners sell their products throughout the world.

Rick has also had success in his own entrepreneurial pursuits ranging from co-owning a franchise to launching his own music production company which resulted in national press and radio play, for children's music that he composed and performed. He used the music to raise funds for children's oriented non-profits in the Seattle area.

As a successful salesperson, sales manager, marketer, corporate executive, and entrepreneur, Rick learned from his own experiences and from the incredibly successful business leaders with whom he's been blessed to work. He has documented his learnings about successful selling in his book, *Winning Lifelong Customers with The Five Abilities*®.

Rick also serves as an advisor to the CEO/Founder of Simplicity Consulting, a marketing consulting firm that has been named to the Inc 5000, five years in a row, as one of the fastest growing private companies in the United States. He also serves on the Board of Directors for Vision House, a non-profit company that serves homeless custodial parents with children in King County, Washington.

In his spare time, Rick enjoys music, both listening and playing. He enjoys sports of all kinds but mainly football and baseball. He's been married to his best friend since 1981. Their son works in the high-end restaurant business in NYC and has entrepreneurial ventures of his own. Their daughter works at Amazon in their digital media business.

Rick is also an MBA graduate of University of Washington's Foster School of Business.

CPSIA information can be obtained
at www.ICGtesting.com
Printed in the USA
FSOW01n0202270317
32217FS

9 781935 953746